(continued from front flap)

richness, and (6) drawing implications. Readers will find here a concrete guide that offers advice about what works and what doesn't.

This approach is invaluable for future research. New pieces of work in a field can be designed to more effectively add to existing knowledge, and programmatic research designs can be developed more efficiently in a world of scarce research resources.

Meta-Analysis in Marketing

About MSI

Founded in 1961, the Marketing Science Institute (MSI) is a nonprofit center for research in marketing. Supported by major corporations for the purpose of advancing marketing practice and knowledge, the Institute brings together the interests and resources of industry and academia to address issues of key importance to marketing. Individual topic areas are identified for study by the Institute's Board of Trustees, representing member companies and the academic community.

Member companies reflect the marketing activities and research needs of a wide variety of consumer and industrial product and service businesses. MSI's academic relationships are also broadly based. Leading researchers from many schools are involved in MSI research. Normally, some 40 to 50 schools are represented at any given time among the researchers who are engaged in some aspect of MSI research.

The Institute conducts research and disseminates research results to the business and academic communities through its workshops, conferences, mini-conferences, and steering group meetings as well as through its publication series. The Institute also issues a Newsletter and Research Briefs that call attention to projects and research findings of interest.

The Marketing Science Institute's primary source of financial support comes from the 40 individual companies that are members of the Institute. The Institute also receives funding through grants from government agencies, foundations, and associations.

The books published jointly by MSI and Lexington Books include:

Effective Television Advertising: A Study of 1000 Commercials, by David W. Stewart and David H. Furse

The Bibliography of Marketing Research Methods, by John R. Dickinson

Meta-Analysis in Marketing: Generalization of Response Models, by John U. Farley and Donald R. Lehmann

Meta-Analysis in Marketing

Generalization of Response Models

John U. Farley
Donald R. Lehmann
Columbia University

Lexington Books
D.C. Heath and Company/Lexington, Massachusetts/Toronto

Library of Congress Cataloging-in-Publication Data

Farley, John U.
  Meta-analysis in marketing.

  1. Marketing research. 2. Meta-analysis. I. Lehmann, Donald R. II. Title.
HF5415.2.F28   1986   658.8'3   86-45606
ISBN 0-669-14039-2 (alk. paper)

Published simultaneously in Canada
Printed in the United States of America
Casebound International Standard Book Number: 0-669-14039-2
Library of Congress Catalog Card Number: 86-45606

The paper used in this publication meets the minimum requirements of American National
Standard for Information Sciences—Permanence of Paper for Printed Library Materials, ANSI
Z39.48-1984. ∞ ™

86 87 88 89 90   8 7 6 5 4 3 2 1

To John Howard. Someday we hope to think as broadly and creatively as he does.

Contents

List of Figures

List of Tables

Preface

The germ of the idea for this book was born longer ago than we choose to admit when we tried to figure out what we had learned from developing two or three simultaneous equation models of consumer behavior. We could not figure out how to do this, though we continued to think it was a good idea.

Mike Ryan came to our rescue, suggesting that we try to generalize about a better-developed field; this collaboration led to our first piece of meta-analysis dealing with parameters of Fishbein models. Gert Assmus then helped us through a meta-analysis of selected parameters in the econometric advertising literature. We are deeply indebted to both Mike and Gert for helping us get back to our original task: generalizing about parameter estimates in the consumer behavior models.

As we proceeded in this stream of work, we realized three things. First, many people seemed to want to know more about how to do a meta-analysis—the steps, what works and what does not, the useful tricks, and so on. Second, we realized that a meta-analytic way of thinking, once developed, leads to a constant urge to generalize, a tendency that came to annoy our friends, colleagues, and students. Finally, to our surprise, meta-analytic thinking, which now seems to us so natural, does not seem so natural to others and in fact has sworn enemies. These three realizations provide the main reasons why we prepared this book. In order to be concrete rather than abstract, we concentrated on our own work; besides, it was easier. We tried to reflect on both the techniques and on our thinking processes as we proceeded through the steps of the meta-analyses. We also try to show specifically why our meta-analyses add to the store of knowledge, in hope that even the sworn enemies may be swayed.

The process of meta-analysis has been extraordinarily creative and helpful to us in designing our own research and in evaluating the work of others. We hope readers find our thoughts equally useful, at least in helping to avoid the labor-intensive way we learned about meta-analysis.

We are grateful to Maxine Braiterman for her timely and accurate help in manuscript preparation and to Kris Lehmann for careful reading of the manuscript. We are also grateful to John Howard, to whom we are pleased to dedicate this book on his "retirement." It was his work on buyer behavior and insatiable search for general models that really got this book started.

* * *

The authors gratefully acknowledge permission to use the following material: "Patterns in Parameters of Buyer Behavior Models: Generalizing from Sparse Replication" by John U. Farley, Donald R. Lehmann, and Michael J. Ryan, *Marketing Science*, 1, no. 2 (Spring 1982):181–204 and "A Working System Model of Car Buyer Behavior" by John U. Farley, J.A. Howard, and Donald R. Lehmann, *Management Science*, 23, no. 3 (November 1976):235–247, published by The Institute of Management Sciences, 290 Westminster Street, Providence, RI 02903; "Decomposition of the Correlation Matrix in Panel Data" by Donald R. Lehmann and John U. Farley, in *Advances in Consumer Research*, 8 (1981), published by the Association for Consumer Research; "Parameter Stationarity and 'Carry-Over Effects' in a Consumer Decision Process Model" by John U. Farley, Donald R. Lehmann, Russell S. Winer, and Jerrold Katz, *Journal of Consumer Research*, 8 (March 1982):465–471; "How Advertising Affects Sales: Meta-Analysis of Econometric Results" by Gert Assmus, John U. Farley, and Donald R. Lehmann, *Journal of Marketing Research*, 21 (February 1984):65–74, published by the American Marketing Association; "Responses to Advertising Contraceptives" by T.R.L. Black and John U. Farley, *Journal of Advertising Research*, 17, no. 5 (October 1977):49–56, published by the Advertising Research Foundation; and "Generalizing from 'Imperfect' Replication" by John U. Farley, Donald R. Lehmann, and Michael J. Ryan, *Journal of Business*, 54, no. 4 (October 1981):597–610, published by The University of Chicago Press.

Meta-Analysis in Marketing

1

An Introduction to Meta-Analysis

This book deals with how quantitative generalizations about market response can be drawn from results of a series of related studies using a process often referred to as meta-analysis. The essence of meta-analysis is comparison of similar but not necessarily identical estimates of quantities measured in different settings—that is, under various treatments in a sort of natural experimental design. Our goal is to use examples of applications of meta-analysis to explore means by which:

Literature review can be made more useful both substantively and for the design of future research.

Accumulated knowledge can be summarized quantitatively.

Systematic sources of differences in results can be identified.

Interesting new hypotheses can be developed.

New pieces of work in a field can be designed to add more effectively to the extant body of that knowledge.

Programmatic research design can be developed more efficiently in a world of scarce research resources.

The book has several motivations. First and foremost is our feeling that the classic literature review is often not as helpful as it should be. Consider the following discussion, which is typical of many literature reviews: "In 1957, Smith said the effect of income on purchase was A. In 1961, Jones said B. In 1964, Baker replicated both Smith and Jones but subsequently (1967) argued for C. Since the methods used were not identical, we cannot be sure whether A, B, or C is true." The statements do not make clear what, if anything, has been learned about the impact of income on purchases. Yet given the availability of quantitative measures such as income elasticities from a set of studies, some quantitative measure of impact should be deducible.

A second motivation comes from the fact that replications of existing work in the social sciences, unlike the physical sciences, are often unrewarded (unpublishable) or not feasible because conditions cannot be recreated. As a result, it is not likely that large numbers of exact replications will ever be available, so some literature-based substitute is required.

A third motivation for attempting to glean quantitative generalizations from past studies comes from the feeling that in some areas, new studies seem to add little to the current state of knowledge. In the area of mail survey response, for example, another study on the topic of colored versus white paper seems at best uninteresting. Summarizing the accumulated wisdom in the preceding 300 studies seems more useful than performing one more of the same type.

A fourth motivation for pursuing a quantitative approach to summarizing past studies is a tendency for authors to play with data seeking significance. For example, if a number of studies produce a correlation as a key measure of output, it seems natural to compare these correlations and to try to explain what makes some of them larger than others. The logical outgrowth of this approach is to treat correlation coefficients as dependent variables and whatever differed across the studies as independent variables in some sort of statistical analysis. This is exactly the approach recommended and discussed throughout much of the remainder of this book.

A final motivation, somewhat specific to marketing, is that many studies are carried out at high expense with little likelihood of their ever being done again. Complex field experiments, for example, are seldom repeated. The ability to glean the maximum quantitative implications from the few existing studies might have significant economic payoff.

Ways to Generalize

There are several available approaches to generalizing results from a set of existing studies. As knowledge about a field develops, the methods are often used in approximately the order in which we present them. We believe that most of these approaches have been useful in marketing but that analytical generalization is just coming into its own in the field.

Classic Literature Review

A literature review has a deservedly important role to play in advancing knowledge, particularly when there are relatively few studies in a field. A literature review also has the advantage of retaining textural content from the studies because it is relatively easy to handle qualitative factors. Classic reviews of well-developed fields such as those by Kassarjian (1971) on personality, Wells (1975) on life-styles, and Wilkie and Pessemier (1973) on multi-attribute attitude models are widely cited and used, although there are regrettably few classics of this type. They also tend to age quickly when work in a field is active. This book hopes to show a way to make them more useful while not losing the insights that are often gained from careful and informed reviews.

Literature reviews often list studies in an area and contrast them in terms of methods, results, and other factors. Examples are Salipante, Notz, and Bigelow's (1982) study of literature reviews, Clarke's (1976) study of advertising effects, Bolton and Chapman's (1984) summary of structural equation modeling, Reibstein, Bateson, and Boulding's (1983) work on conjoint analysis, Bass et al. (1984) on the order of the choice process, and Kalwani and Silk (1982) on purchase intention measures. Conclusions about the general nature of the results are often drawn by inspection. Meta-analysis often starts with such summary data, using predictive models (for example, ANOVA) to assess the overall average result and to identify sources of systematic differences in results across studies.

Aggregation of p-Values

One of the earliest forms of statistical generalization was to estimate the significance level of a particular effect. These procedures basically use a weighted average approach where the weights depend on the sample size and/or the reliability of the measures in each of the studies. One recent example of this approach in marketing dealt with combining significance levels in test marketing (Dutka, 1984).

Although these studies are interesting, their focus is on statistical significance per se. Since significance is, among other things, a function of sample size (almost anything is significant given a large enough sample and almost nothing is significant given a small one), it seems to be of secondary concern. Our approach to meta-analysis focuses instead on the best available estimate of the magnitude of an effect rather than its statistical significance.

Averaging and/or Counting

In a research tradition related to aggregating p-values, a number of researchers have addressed the issue of aggregating effects across several studies. The aggregation usually involves some sort of averaging or construction of frequency distributions.

Many examples of this approach appear in the marketing literature. For example, Yu and Cooper (1983) produce average response rates for a number of mail survey methods. The work on marketing responses by Shultz and Leone (1980), on life-style traits by Lastovicka (1982), and on return postage by Armstrong and Lusk (1985) are other examples of this approach. Examples, however, come from many different areas, as Fishburn and Kochenberger's (1979) analysis of Von Neumann-Morgenstern utility functions demonstrates.

In spirit, this approach is much closer to the method recommended in this book since it focuses on magnitude of impact rather than significance. It differs, however, in that it basically treats interstudy differences as nuisances or inconveniences that should be covered up by the averaging or counting process. Averaging thus assumes that the systematic effects in the natural experiment that produces the available results can reasonably be treated as random error whose systematic effect can be removed by averaging. By contrast, meta-analysis attempts to treat identifiable systematic differences in studies as factors in a natural experimental design—that is, as part of the findings rather than nuisances.

Programmed Research

A handful of research programs in marketing have extended over a long period of time, amassing considerable corroborative (though not strictly replicative) evidence of consistency of results. Probably the most extensive is that of Andrew Ehrenberg and his collaborators, who have fit various probability distributions to patterns of choice in consumer and industrial markets with consistent results (Charlton 1973; Chatfield, Ehrenberg, and Goodhardt 1966; Chatfield and Goodhardt 1970, 1973, 1975; Ehrenberg 1959, 1965, 1972, 1975; Ehrenberg and Goodhardt 1970, 1976, 1979; Goodhardt 1976; Goodhardt and Chatfield 1973; Goodhardt, Ehrenberg, and Collins 1975; Kau and Ehrenberg 1984). The results are particularly consistent for arrays of brand choice and store choice under relatively stable conditions.

Somewhat more broadly cast programs involving various sets of linked computer models include work by Little (1975), Urban (1970, 1975), Urban and Katz (1983), Hauser and Gaskin (1984), and Hauser and Shugan (1983). Included are various families of models: BRANDAID for brand management, SPRINTER and PERCEPTOR for analyses of new products, and DEFENDER for analysis of defensive strategies in more mature markets.

Research programs such as these, unfortunately, are few and far between. Meta-analysis offers an alternative approach to assessing consistency in more loosely related studies, particularly where real programmatic research is absent.

Triangulation

Triangulation integrates findings by studying convergence of estimates or conclusions from several studies. If different sampling or data collection techniques in two or more studies produce either similar or explainably different estimates or findings, convergent validity might be established. Triangulation is useful with small sets of studies in which methods and findings are reported completely (Sternthal, Tybout, and Calder 1986).

Like the traditional literature review, triangulation depends on the researcher's judgment and ability to conceptualize, compare, and interpret findings. It becomes clumsy as the number of studies becomes large because of the large numbers of potential combinations that must be assessed. Further, triangulation offers no means to produce probability statements about resulting generalizations.

Analytical Generalization

The approach of this book is best described as analytical generalization, defined in this way: "The approach to research integration referred to as meta-analysis is nothing more than the attitude of data analysis applied to quantitative summaries or individual experiments" (Glass, McGaw, and Smith 1981, p. 21).

Analytical generalization requires that a key output or outputs of the studies being examined be quantitative. It also requires a sufficient number of observations so that numerical analysis is worthwhile. It is also useful if the key output(s) is (are) in comparable scale units. For this reason, any of the following are useful analyses for meta-analyses: fit measures (for example, R^2, U, Wilks lambda), sensitivity measures (for example, beta coefficients, correlations of various orders, elasticities), and percentages and proportions (for example, response rates). A single reported study may furnish multiple observations.

Provided it occurs in more than one case, anything identifiable that varies systematically between observations can be used as an independent variable and consequently tested to see whether it has an impact on the dependent variable. Although numerous independent variables can be used, we have found that most fall into four broad categories:

1. Model specification (such as variables included and functional form of a model).

2. Research environment (such as who was studied, what the study was about, why the study was conducted, when the study was conducted, or where the study was conducted).

3. Measurement (such as semantic differential versus constant sum scales or time series of various measurement periods).

4. Estimation methods (such as ordinary least squares, two-stage least squares, or more exotic methods).

A number of authors have produced major works in the general area of meta-analysis, including Glass, McGaw, and Smith (1981), Hedges and Olkin (1985), and Hunter, Schmidt, and Jackson (1982). A number of marketing applications have also begun to appear, including a session at the 1983 Association for Consumer Research meeting that featured papers by Reilly and Conover; Monroe and Krishnan; Houston, Peter, and Sawyer; and Ryan and Barclay. Work on rating scales by Churchill and Peter (1984), on salesmen performance (Churchill et al. 1985), and on effect sizes (Peterson, Albaum, and Beltramini 1985) has also appeared recently. This book extends these works with special emphasis on marketing response models.

How Meta-Analysis and Replication Relate

Much of the criticism of meta-analysis is due to a misunderstanding of what it seeks to accomplish. Meta-analysis, replication, and testing of competing models generally have quite different goals:

	How Done?	*Goal*
Replication	Same model, same data	Reliability of results in the same situation
Testing competing models	Different models, same data	Robustness of results to alternative model specifications; search for best model
Meta-analysis	Different models, different data	Generalizability of results to new situations

Meta-analysis is, of course, the general case. Meta-analysis applied to several batches of data collected in the same way and involving the same model is replication, and there is no reason why such replication cannot be built into general meta-analysis if a set of studies includes some replications. Testing competing models on the same data is really a within-study type of meta-analysis, and general meta-analysis often incorporates multiple results from a given study.

The reaction to meta-analysis as we promote it is usually a combination of curiosity (as in, "Have they lost their minds?") and disbelief (as in, "Don't they know that you can't combine apples and oranges?"). In fact, much of the criticism is of the form "If it isn't 'precise' [which it is not], then it can't be useful." We counter by suggesting that if something is exactly precise, it is likely to deal with a relatively small area.

If we were to argue that meta-analysis is the only way to advance knowledge, then these criticisms would be both warranted and probably charitable. Our contention, however, is that meta-analysis is a useful approach that, if properly integrated with induction-case study, modeling work, and careful empirical research in both laboratory and field settings, can increase knowledge.

By increasing knowledge, we mean uncovering both general rules and subtleties. Meta-analysis clearly focuses on uncovering general rules. It may also, however, uncover a subtle result in the form of a factor that systematically affects results, which we would not a priori have thought mattered. When such findings occur, they are neither causal nor conclusive. Rather, they suggest a pattern that merits further assessment. Thus, a meta-analysis at once summarizes (in terms of the average results) and spurs further work (in terms of identifiable systematic differences).

Meta-Analyzing Marketing

Marketing can be meta-analyzed at many levels. For example, managers are often interested in reasons why populations of potential buyers consume such different amounts of a product, even though they have apparently comparable ability to purchase the product. For example yogurt is purchased by nearly 90 percent of the households in some European countries and by less than 5 percent in others. It is possible to compare consumption levels, attitude levels, and levels of satisfaction for different populations for a given product, for different products for a given population, or both. Analysis of reasons for different response rates to mail questionnaires involves meta-analysis in this spirit. Meta-analysis is particularly useful for analysis of patterns of response of populations to external stimuli, particularly those under control of the marketer, such as price, advertising, or distribution. Analysis of differences in response is the subject of this book. The reasons are both theoretical and substantive. On a theoretical level, scaleless price and advertising elasticities can be compared directly to assess market responsiveness to controllable (price and advertising) or uncontrollable (income) factors on market response. Budgeting and forecasting implications follow directly, as do implications for long-term and short-term pricing policies. More fundamental, elasticities are linked together in an equilibrium relationship (Dorfmann and Steiner 1954) that provides a sound theoretical basis for comparing them. Substantively, meta-analysis of response is particularly useful because studies of market response are difficult and expensive, and they are also relatively rare. They tend to be done under fairly specific and controlled conditions, which ordinarily differ over studies. Meta-analysis can provide predictions for a new set of circumstances by developing partial estimates for each element of the new study based on similar elements of existing studies. For example, a study of the impact of advertising on a durable in Europe may benefit from results of other studies of durables elsewhere and from results in studies of advertising of other products in Europe.

Plan of the Book

Our approach to meta-analysis is to view a body of literature in the context of a natural, uncontrolled experiment. The experimental design will almost always be imperfect relative to classic experimental designs, and the result of these imperfections (correlated factors, small sample sizes, and so on) occupies a good deal of our attention in this book. In fact, absent these imperfections in the natural experimental design, meta-analysis would be a relatively simple process of averaging or (at worst) feeding data into a well-structured computer program.

Meta-analysis generally proceeds in the six identifiable but somewhat overlapping steps shown in figure 1–1, which also constitutes the outline of the book. Each step consumes approximately the same amount of researchers' time, although the activities involved at each step are somewhat different. Often work at one step sends the researcher back to an earlier step for reformulation, so there is some cycling.

Step 1:   Construct the dependent variable for the meta-analysis
(Ch. 2)   Collect results
                 Express results in comparable units

Step 2:   Identify the theoretically important elements of the natural
(Ch. 3)   experiment in research environment as the independent
             variables for the meta-analysis
                 Environmental differences
                 Differences in measurement
                 Differences in estimation process

Step 3:   Analyze the natural experiment for
(Ch. 4)   Singularity
                 Particularly harmful non-orthogonality
                 Extreme imbalance
                 Limitations in degrees of freedom

Step 4:   Perform the classic meta-analysis
(Ch. 5)   Building meta-analytic elements into the model
                 Direct decomposition of correlation matrices
                 Multivariate analysis of variance
                 Analysis of variance

Step 5:   Experiment with methods to deal with defects in the natural
(Ch. 6)   experiment
                 Partitioning of shared explained variance
                 Gestalt formation
                 Causal and precedence analysis

Step 6:   Draw implications
(Ch. 7)   For available information
                 For new studies

Figure 1–1. Steps in the Meta-Analysis Process

In meta-analysis, as in many other kinds of research, there is a tendency to jump directly to the analysis itself (step 4) with subsequent waste of time and energy. In particular, step 2 (identification of the theoretically important elements of the natural experiment) and step 3 (assessment of empirical characteristics of the experimental design) should be done carefully and painstakingly. Otherwise a myriad of problems at step 4, the meta-analysis, will necessitate the return to steps 2 and 3 until they have been executed satisfactorily. Step 5, which is highly experimental, involves attempts to get more richness from the results—for example, by decomposing nested effects and incorporating precedence and causation. The drawing of implications has, in our experience, been a rather lengthy process, requiring continual reexamination of conclusions in the light of discovery of new results or of questions by colleagues and readers.

For illustration, we draw mainly on four examples of meta-analysis of response models that represent different situations in terms of context, model, and measurement:

1. A study of thirty-seven applications of the extended Fishbein behavioral intention model (Farley, Lehmann, and Ryan 1981). This uses a well-structured literature with a relatively large population of studies, all of which basically use the same model containing the same response parameters.

2. A study of 128 econometric advertising models (Assmus, Farley, and Lehmann 1984). These models differ in many important ways, and there are a large number of differences over the studies and over the research environments. The models, however, contain certain common response parameters.

3. A study of 4 system models of buyer behavior (Farley, Lehmann, and Ryan 1982). This handful of highly dissimilar models allows us to examine meta-analysis under difficult circumstances. In particular, major efforts are needed to reduce the problem to manageable size and to pool response parameters to make meta-analysis feasible.

4. A tracking study involving introduction of a new automobile (Farley, Howard, and Lehmann 1976). Results of work in context of a four-equation model are used primarily to illustrate incorporation of meta-analytic parametric variables directly into the process of estimating response in a single study in order to assess parameter differences across brands, over time, over markets, and so forth.

We use these examples because we are familiar with their inner workings and because we think they offer a range of problems faced in formal meta-analysis. In all cases, analysis is based on scaleless versions of response parameters derived from these four models. Detailed descriptions of measurement are available in each of the publications cited, and we pay little attention to measurement issues in this book. Each meta-analysis is divided into pieces that are discussed in chapters 2 through 6 in terms of the issues shown in figure 1–1. To get a coherent picture of any one of the studies, we suggest referring to the original paper.

In each chapter, we proceed from meta-analyses that are relatively simple and involve well-structured models and data sets (the Fishbein models generally provide this illustration) to meta-analyses that require much more complex sequences of analysis and much more judgment in design (the buyer behavior models usually provide this example).

2
The Setting of Meta-Analysis: Identifying Studies and Constructing the Dependent Variable(s)

The first step in meta-analysis is the identification of a body of studies that have a comparable variable worth generalizing about. This step requires considerable care and thought. It also requires patience to search thoroughly. In general, meta-analysis must wait until enough evidence, published and unpublished, exists in a field to provide a reasonable sample size of response parameters. This leads to a possible publication bias since there is a tendency for only those studies with statistically significant results that are consistent with an accepted paradigm to be available. On occasion a sample of studies is actively sought (such as Cattin and Wittink's 1983 study of conjoint analysis applications or Wiseman's 1979 study of response rates), but these suffer from attendant nonresponse and response bias problems.

The question of when meta-analysis is feasible can generally be answered only after some attempt is made to assemble a set of dependent variables. The basic working role about how many observations are needed is subject to fairly conventional sample size considerations, involving the relationship between the number of available data points and the number of inferences to be made. For example, five exact replications of a study should provide quite good average estimates of model parameters; a set of studies that differ in four or five different important respects will require at least twenty studies, with some representing each of the key interstudy differences for reasonable inference. We have found two important points in assembling the dependent variables for several meta-analyses. First, most literatures are rather small. This means that there are always fewer studies available than anticipated, so it is important not to get discouraged; even a dozen semicomparable studies will probably be useful. Second, a given study will often provide more than one observation because differently specified models are fit for different products, markets, or segments. A book like Comanor and Wilson (1974) is an example. While using multiple observations from a single study may pose problems for inference, there will generally be more models than studies available.

The set of estimates from the collected studies provides the observations on the dependent variable or variables for the meta-analysis. Estimates from various different studies ordinarily are not available in directly comparable units due to differences in measurement or in estimation methodology. Response parameters, however, can usually be expressed as or converted to a correlation coefficient of some order, an elasticity, or a beta coefficient. Some sort of "normalized" measure may also be developed that avoids inappropriate comparison of utilities over subjects or over studies (Bass and Wilkie 1973).

Choice of the dependent variable set is based on theoretical and practical grounds. The set should contain variables of substantive importance to the field under study, and it must have been measured a reasonable number of times. For example, the coefficients of labor and capital are important in the study of production functions in economics. Over a hundred applications of the Cobb-Douglas model are available, while only a handful of more complex models (with varying elasticities or constant elasticities of substitution) are available (Farley, Lehmann, and Oliva 1985).

The remainder of the chapter deals with collecting studies and identifying dependent variables in the four studies used as examples throughout this book.

Meta-Analysis in a Set of Studies Based on the Same Method and Model: Patterns of Parameter Estimates in Tests of Fishbein's Behavioral Intention Model

Studies based on the Fishbein model of behavioral intention are numerous and have similar structures in terms of both measurement and analysis. They provide a good first illustration of developing the dependent variable for meta-analysis.

The Fishbein Model

The central equation in Fishbein and Ajzen's theory (1975) is

$$BI = (A_{act})\omega_1 + (SN)\omega_2$$

where ω_1 and ω_2 are empirically determined standardized regression coefficients (beta weights) directly comparable over studies. Measures of goodness of fit of the model are similarly scaleless and comparable.

Variables are defined as follows: BI = behavioral intention; A_{act} = attitude toward behavioral act, which may be measured directly or computed as

$$\sum_{i=1}^{k} B_i a_i$$

where B is the probability that the performance of a specific behavior will lead to an ith outcome, a_i is the positive or negative evaluation of the ith outcome, and k is the number of salient outcomes; SN = the subjective norm, which can also either be measured directly or computed as

$$\sum_{j=1}^{k} NB_j MC_j$$

where NB_j is the probability that the performance of a specific behavior is expected by a jth group or individual, MC_j is the motivation to comply or not to comply with the expectation of the jth group or individual, and k is the number of salient groups or individuals.

Dependent Variables for Meta-Analysis of Fishbein Results

Values of ω_1, ω_2, and $\bar{R}$ (to measure goodness of fit), available from every study, are ideal dependent variables for meta-analysis. Twenty-six published studies reported thirty-seven tests of Fishbein's model that incorporated comparable measurement and parameter estimation. Each produced a set of the three parameters. Sample sizes ranged from 20 to 282, averaging 103, with means, standard deviations, and ranges as indicated in table 2–1. Sign and t-tests indicate a significant positive value for $\bar{\omega}_1$, $\bar{\omega}_2$, and $\bar{R}$. All three parameters were also statistically different from zero in most individual cases. This means that statistical tests in future applications should be based on anticipated results other than on zero-value null hypotheses. Part of the value of meta-analysis involves providing nonzero null values for future tests.

Table 2–1
Summary Statistics from Fishbein Models

	$\bar{\omega}_1$	$\bar{\omega}_2$	$\bar{R}$
Mean	0.450	0.301	0.709
Standard deviation	0.216	0.227	0.124
Range	−0.15 to 0.75	−0.03 to 0.95	0.600 to 0.940
Interquartile range	0.27 to 0.64	0.21 to 0.55	0.670 to 0.840
Number positive	36	36	

Source: Reprinted with permission from John U. Farley, Donald R. Lehmann, and Michael J. Ryan, "Generalizing from 'Imperfect' Replication," *Journal of Business*, 54, no. 4, (October 1981), The University of Chicago Press, © 1981 by the University of Chicago. All rights reserved.

Meta-Analysis of Comparable Parameters from Noncomparable Models: Advertising Elasticities

Econometric studies of advertising in the context of a general demand function have become quite common over the past two decades and were in fact among the earliest applications of econometrics to marketing problems (Telser 1962; Palda 1964).

Econometric Modeling of Advertising

A rather broad operationalization of a demand function, which involves elements contained in most models, incorporates current advertising, an advertising carryover effect through a lagged dependent variable, other elements of the marketing mix, and exogenous factors is

$$Q_i = \beta_0 + \beta_1 A_i + \beta_2 Q_{i,t\text{-}1} + \beta_3 P_i + \sum_{j=4}^{h} \beta_j X_i + u_i \qquad (2.1)$$

where Q_i is a sales or share measure and $Q_{i,t\text{-}1}$ its lagged value; A_i is an advertising volume or share measure; P_i is price; the X_i's are appropriately defined exogenous variables; and u_i is a stochastic error term.

In the most common time-series form, the subscript i refers to time t. In multiplicative models (in which the variables are measured in logarithms), the regression coefficients are scaleless elasticities assumed constant over the range of the function. In linear models, elasticities can be estimated by multiplying β_i by the ratio of the means of the respective explanatory and dependent variable in order to convert them into units of common measure whose sensitivities can be compared over studies, at least at the means of the two variables.

Unlike the Fishbein models, there is great variation in model specification in the econometric advertising literature. This gives rise to an interesting logical problem in making comparisons of models related to what is meant by a correct model. For example, if one model specification appropriately encompasses all situations (product, time frame, setting, and so forth) and various underspecified models are estimated, bias will result. On the other hand, bias and multicollinearity may result if variables extraneous to a given application are included. We use a relatively complete model as the basis for the meta-analysis and the effects of more or less full specifications are assessed analytically.

Dependent Variables for Meta-Analysis of Econometric Advertising Models

Although econometric advertising models differ materially in specification as well as in setting, they contain certain common elements, which form the dependent variables for this meta-analysis:

Short-term advertising effect (β_1) is an element of every model.

Goodness of fit measured by a coefficient of determination (R^2) is available for most models.

Advertising carryover, which links short-term to long-term elasticities, is explicitly specified in most cases.

In the case of the commonly used Koyck distributed lag specification, for example,

$$\text{long-term } \eta_a = \frac{\text{short-term } \eta_a}{(1-\lambda)}$$

where λ is β_2 in equation 2.1.

This meta-analysis was performed on estimated parameters from 128 models reported in twenty-two studies published before 1981. Because carryover was not specified in all models and the coefficient of determination was not always reported, sample sizes differ for the three dependent variables and the three measures must be analyzed separately. In the case of multiplicative models, the coefficients were elasticities; in the case of linear models, elasticities were estimated by multiplying the relevant regression coefficient by the ratio of the means of the dependent variable and the advertising measure.

Overall the distributions of the estimated parameters summarized in table 2–2 are plausible. Equilibrium short-term elasticities should be greater than zero (negative values imply negative returns to advertising) and less than one (values greater than unity imply increasing returns to scale of advertising and hence imply the firm is underadvertising). In fact, only one of the 128 estimated elasticities is less than zero, and none is greater than one. Similarly, the coefficient of the lagged dependent variable should be between zero and one, and all values of the estimates are within this range. There is, however, considerable interstudy variability in all three measures. Part of this wide range in the three parameters may be due to variation over studies in model structure, measurement, and research environment. Unlike the Fishbein models, the econometric advertising models differ fundamentally in terms of specification of variables other than

Table 2–2
Summary of Statistics on Advertising Elasticities, Carryover Effects, and Goodness of Fit from 128 Econometric Models

	Mean*	Standard Deviation	Available Sample Size
Short-term elasticity (β_1)	0.221	0.264	128
Carryover (β_2)	0.468	0.306	114
R^2	0.783	0.214	109

Source: Reprinted with permission from Gert Assmus, John U. Farley, and Donald R. Lehmann, "How Advertising Affects Sales: A Meta-Analysis of Econometric Results," *Journal of Marketing Research*, 21, no. 1 (February 1984), published by the American Marketing Association.
*All significantly greater than zero at $\alpha = 0.01$.

advertising and in terms of specification of the pattern of how advertising affects sales over time. Although the estimates are scaleless elasticities or can be converted easily into elasticities, problems of comparability arise because some models are built on brands and others on products, and some models use market shares and others sales volume as independent variables. Also, research contexts differ in many ways: products, geographic location, definitions of dependent and explanatory variables, estimation methods, measurement time frame, and others.

Meta-Analysis and Sparse Replication: Four Buyer Behavior Models

Analyzing patterns in results from buyer behavior systems models, such as those based on the Howard and Sheth (1969) theory, involves more severe problems. First, few studies are available, so sample sizes of a given parameter are uselessly small, and some means for aggregating parameters is necessary. Second, output measures are not directly comparable due to important differences over the studies in model specifications and in measurement procedures. Third, applications differ in terms of product and situation. Fourth, parameter estimation procedures differ. As a result, meta-analysis of these results requires more steps of analysis and assumptions more heroic than those required in meta-analysis of either the Fishbein or econometric studies.

Buyer Behavior Models

The buyer behavior models are specified in the form of flowcharts such as the one in figure 2–1, which is the model used to analyze results of a contraceptive test market in Kenya (Black and Farley 1977).

The endogenous variables used here are from a set of five core variables identified as having theoretical justification, valid operational measures, and potential usefulness in managerial decision making. Based on these criteria, working versions of consumer behavior models have been reduced in practice to the following endogenous variables: awareness or attention; knowledge; attitude; trial, intention, or purchase; and satisfaction. The Kenyan model in figure 2–1 contains three of these five variables.

Specification of relationships among pairs of endogenous variables, which form the central variable structure of each application, varies across studies. Attention or awareness, intention or behavior, and knowledge appear in all four studies, attitude appears in three, and satisfaction appears in two. The endogenous variables play the dual roles of dependent and explanatory variable; for example, attitude can be a dependent variable and can also be causal for one of the other endogenous variables. Problems related to using scale measurements such as attitude and intention in meta-analysis are discussed in detail in Farley, Lehmann, and Ryan (1982).

Specifications of exogenous variables also vary over studies, chiefly because

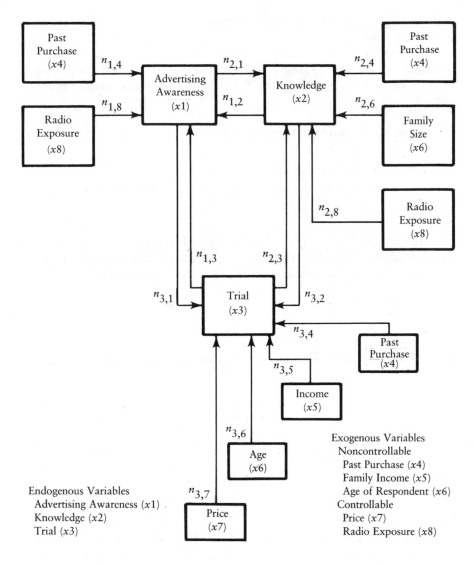

Figure 2–1. Elasticities Contributed by Each Wave of the Kenyan Contraceptive Study

of specific market characteristics. The exogenous variables are of two sorts: controllable, including price, distribution, and advertising, and uncontrollable (chiefly sociodemographic) measures relevant in a particular market. Only exogenous variables that are not idiosyncratic to a particular study can be used in a meta-analysis, although some grouping of similar variables (for example, various measures of wealth or income) into more or less homogeneous groups is possible.

*The Dependent Variables for Meta-Analysis of Buyer
Behavior Results*

Regression coefficients linking pairings in twenty prespecified linear models from the following four published studies provide the dependent variables for the meta-analysis:

1. A convenience food product (Farley and Ring 1970, as modified in Farley and Ring 1971, 1972).
2. A personal care product (Farley, Howard, and Lehmann 1974).
3. Subcompact automobiles (Farley, Howard, and Lehmann 1976).
4. A contraceptive (Black and Farley 1977).

Research designs (table 2–3) involved both panels and repeated waves of fresh samples. The studies differ in terms of size of the variable set, setting, type of product, and statistical approaches used in parameter estimation.

Table 2–3
Key Features of Data Collection for Research on Buyer Behavior Models

| Product | Setting | Number of Variables in the System | | | Stage of Product in Development Cycle | Data Collected Specifically for Systems Models |
		Endogenous	Exogenous	Total		
Convenience food product	U.S.	11	17	28	Test market	No
Personal product	Argentina	10	18	28	Test market	Yes
Contraceptive	Kenya	3	6	9	Test market	No
Automobiles	U.S.	4	8	12	National introduction	No

Source: Reprinted by permission from "Patterns in Parameters of Buyer Behavior Models: Generalizing from Sparse Replication," John U. Farley, Donald R. Lehmann, and Michael J. Ryan, *Marketing Science*, 1, no. 2 (Spring 1982), Copyright 1982, The Institute of Management Sciences, 290 Westminster Street, Providence, RI 02903.

As was indicated in figure 2–1, the meta-analysis is done after model parameters are converted into scaleless elasticities, so interstudy comparison makes sense. The conversion is:

$$\eta_{ij} = b_{ij}\bar{x}_j/\bar{y}_i$$

where η_{ij} is the elasticity of endogenous dependent variable i with regard to explanatory variable j; b_{ij} is the regression coefficient linking endogenous variable i with explanatory variable j; $\bar{y}_i$ is the mean of endogenous dependent variable i; and $\bar{x}_j$ is the mean of explanatory variable j, which may be endogenous or exogenous. The calculation produces an elasticity estimated at the means of the two involved variables and provides a first approximation that allows comparison in a relatively small neighborhood around the points at which the estimates are made for each study.

Pooling the available elasticities across the four studies and the five endogenous variables produced 113 values with a qualitative pattern of significance. The mean of the nonprice elasticities is 0.28 (significantly greater than 0), and 96 of the original regression coefficients upon which the elasticities were based are positive and significant. All price elasticities are negative and significant as

Number of Waves of Interviews Used	Numbers of Brands Modeled	Sample Size	Type of Research Design	Duration of Measurement Used in Models
1	1	693	Three waves of cross-sectional interviews combined & treated as one sample	3 months
2	1	200	Two-wave panel plus pre-introduction measurements	8 months
2	1	499	Two-waves of cross-sectional samples plus pre-introduction measurements	12 months
4	8	1209	Four-wave panel one pre- and post-introduction measurements	18 months

expected. Despite this evidence of significant model effect, however, there is, as in the first three examples, a broad range of values for the elasticities that might be partially explained by specifics of measurement, estimation, and application.

Meta-Analysis within the Structure of a Single Study: A Multiwave, Multigroup, Multibrand Car Buyer Behavior Model

Meta-analysis is particularly flexible in the context of a single study where comparisons might be made over market segments, brands, time, or markets, for example. Measurement methodology and estimation procedures are generally identical in these circumstances, so raw estimates are often directly comparable. If the raw data are available, the meta-analysis can be built directly into the modeling and the estimation procedures, as is illustrated by the buyer behavior model associated with the automobile study.

Car Buyer Behavior Model

A four-equation consumer behavior model was built to analyze data from a national probability sample of respondents expressing some interest in buying a subcompact car within the next two years. Figure 2–2 shows the four-equation brand-level model, which was assembled using a combination of results of prior studies plus an initial check for consistent patterns in preliminary cross-tabulations and correlations from results of wave 1. The model contains four endogenous and eight exogenous variables.

The endogenous variables are Brand Comprehension (y_1), Confidence in Judgment (y_2), Attitude (y_3), and Intention to Buy the Brand (y_4). Although purchase is clearly the key behavioral variable, intention to purchase serves here as a surrogate for purchase for analysis of this infrequently-purchased durable because very few actual purchases of the product category (subcompact cars) and even fewer of any specific brand occurred during the initial tracking period.

The set of exogenous variables in the model, culled from a much larger set of candidates on the basis of reasonableness and preliminary indications of explanatory power, included Advertising Recall (x_1), Intention to Buy the Product Category (x_2), the Number of Licensed Drivers (x_7) and Young Drivers (x_8) in the household, as well as Age (x_4), Sex (x_3), Income (x_5), and Education (x_6) of the Respondent.

Dependent Variables for Car Buyer Behavior Study

Estimated coefficients of a revised model constitute the dependent variable for the meta-analysis in this case. Table 2–4 summarizes 120 sets of four regressions,

Matrix form:

$$
\begin{bmatrix}
-1 & \beta_{12} & \beta_{13} & \\
 & -1 & & \beta_{24} \\
 & & -1 & \beta_{34} \\
 & & & -1
\end{bmatrix} Y +
\begin{bmatrix}
\gamma_{10} & \gamma_{11} & \gamma_{12} & & \gamma_{15} & & \\
\gamma_{20} & & \gamma_{22} & \gamma_{23} & \gamma_{24} & \gamma_{25} & \gamma_{26} \\
\gamma_{30} & \gamma_{31} & \gamma_{32} & \gamma_{33} & \gamma_{34} & & \gamma_{36} \\
\gamma_{40} & \gamma_{41} & \gamma_{42} & & \gamma_{44} & & \gamma_{46} & \gamma_{47}
\end{bmatrix} X = u \quad (2.2)
$$

Equation form:

$$y_{1t} = \beta_{12}y_{2t} + \beta_{13}y_{3t} + \gamma_{10} + \gamma_{11}x_1 + \gamma_{12}x_2 + \gamma_{15}x_5 + \gamma_{18}x_8 + u_{1t}$$

$$y_{2t} = \beta_{24}y_{4t} \qquad\quad + \gamma_{20} + \gamma_{22}x_2 + \gamma_{23}x_3 + \gamma_{24}x_4 + \gamma_{25}x_5 + \gamma_{26}x_6 + u_{2t}$$

$$(2.2a)$$

$$y_{3t} = \beta_{34}y_{4t} \qquad\quad + \gamma_{30} + \gamma_{32}x_2 + \gamma_{33}x_3 + \gamma_{34}x_4 + \gamma_{36}x_6 + u_{3t}$$

$$y_{4t} = \qquad\qquad\qquad\quad + \gamma_{40} + \gamma_{41}x_1 + \gamma_{42}x_2 + \gamma_{44}x_4 + \gamma_{46}x_6 + \gamma_{47}x_7 + u_{4t}$$

Figure 2–2. Parametric Forms of the Working Model Structure

each run for the following groups: 5 waves, 4 interviewing groups, 3 different brands (deemed most important in terms of consumer interest and including the new brand), and 2 estimation methods: ordinary least squares (OLS) and two-stage least squares (TSLS). Since the sample is relatively large, estimates of individual parameters can be compared directly to one another. Averages of these 120 estimates (5 waves × 4 groups × 3 brands × 2 estimation methods) of each coefficient (table 2–4) suggest several things that constitute the first level of meta-analysis. First, constants are nonzero, which suggests that actual bottom of the scales is not the minimum value of 1, even for the new brand before the introduction. There is no reason to expect people uncertain about a stimulus to rate it at the absolutely minimum value available, and in fact they appear to give it a rating consistent with their average or prototype view of the category.

Second, the signs of coefficient among all the endogenous variables are positive as would be expected, and all but two of the averages of these are significantly different from zero. The coefficients of income and education suggest that the new brand appeals to a low- to moderate-income-level segment, and the coefficient of sex in the confidence equations confirms a prior expectation that this is a product about which males are likely to feel better informed.

Table 2–4
Average Estimated Values of Coefficients from 120 Car Buyer Behavior Models

Dependent	Constant	Predictor	Coef. (SE)	Predictor	Coef. (SE)
Intention =	0.300 (1.606)[a]	(Attitude)	+0.099 (0.072)	(Confidence)	+0.016 (0.031)
		(Recall)	+0.044 (0.007)	(Propensity)	+0.272 (0.012)
		(Income)	−0.021 (0.012)	(Child)	+0.080 (0.078)
Attitude =	3.356 (10.108)	(Brand Comprehension)	+1.412 (1.941)	(Propensity)	+0.082 (0.007)
		(Sex)	+0.416 (0.543)	(Age)	−0.007 (0.012)
		(Income)	−0.120 (0.022)	(Education)	−0.056 (0.011)
Confidence =	4.351 (6.106)	(Brand Comprehension)	+0.252 (1.690)	(Recall)	+0.251 (0.017)
		(Propensity)	+0.035 (0.007)	(Sex)	−0.894 (0.425)
		(Age)	−0.012 (0.008)	(Education)	+0.030 (0.009)
Brand comprehension =	0.886 (0.380)	(Recall)	+0.084 (0.002)	(Propensity)	−0.013 (0.001)
		(Age)	+0.027 (0.002)	(Education)	+0.041 (0.001)
		(Number of Drivers)	0.017 (0.007)		

Source: Reprinted by permission from "A Working System Model of Car Buyer Behavior," John U. Farley, J.A. Howard, and Donald R. Lehmann, *Management Science*, 23, no. 3 (November 1976), Copyright 1976, The Institute of Management Sciences, 290 Westminster Street, Providence, RI 02903.

[a]Coefficients are averaged across all five waves, four groups, three cars per group, and two estimation methods. All the average coefficients are significantly different from 0 at the 95 percent level with the following exceptions: Confidence in Intention equation (90 percent level), Age in the Attitude equation, and Age in the Confidence Equation (80 percent level).

Large differences among these individual averages are indicated by the standard deviations in table 2–4, however, so a more detailed examination of these differences is warranted.

Discussion

Despite the evident comparability within each of the four groups of the studies discussed in this chapter, there are some caveats. First, no collection, however careful, exhausts all studies. Second, any set of studies as a whole in no way represents random selection of products or research settings but rather is a collection of choices made by individual researchers acting more or less independently of one another. These choices are often dominated by such accidents as data availability or the availability of computer programs to do particular types of estimation. Comparing variables measured on scales also may require strong assumptions about both origin and metric of scales, so caution must be exercised.

Further, meta-analysis based on published literature often has a publication bias resulting from the use of studies that have passed a reviewing process and that in general also pass standard classical tests of significance. This tends to bias the effects toward being larger by systematically excluding smaller or nonsignificant results. This practice also tends to encourage a certain acceptable perspective, lessening interstudy variability on key dimensions and increasing collinearity in the meta-analysis by eliminating studies with insignificant or implausible estimates that may make sense in a broader context. Industrial and commercial studies, which are mostly unpublished and often classified, also tend to be excluded.

It is possible, nevertheless, to collect studies suitable to meta-analysis. Here we have been able to construct the requisite estimates of comparable quantities for each of the four sets of studies used as illustrations in this chapter. Some measures are directly comparable in their natural units of measure, while others—correlations, beta coefficients, or elasticities—are scaleless. Still others, measured in noncomparable units, can be converted into elasticities. These measures are the values of the dependent variables for the meta-analysis.

The next chapter turns attention to the design of the natural experiment underlying the meta-analysis—that is, to the independent variables.

3

Interstudy Differences: Identifying Elements of the Natural Experiment as Independent Variables

A natural experimental design composed of key interstudy differences provides the set of independent variables for the meta-analyses. The design will vary from setting to setting, but the designs are likely to share certain general characteristics. This chapter examines examples of how potentially salient differences are modeled to allow analysis of a set of studies.

In most cases, there are good theoretical or established empirical patterns of results to suggest which variables should be in the design. A thorough understanding of the field under study, preferably as a contributor to the field, is also a key requirement for the meta-analyst to be effective at setting up the natural experimental design.

Suggestions for design elements come from several sources. First, most fields have some theoretical structures that may indicate possibly important differences. In buyer behavior models, for example, we might expect more information processing by consumers for new products or for durable products than for familiar brands of packaged goods, so models of the latter may be less responsive to information inputs. Second, heated debates in a field about appropriate measurement are not unusual. For example, alternative ways to measure the attitude and normative variables in the Fishbein models may produce different results. Third, there may be major differences in cultural setting or in the business environment that may cause differences in results. Finally, model specification and estimation procedures may cause some differences in results.

From a meta-analytical point of view, the salient characteristics divide into features of the research environment (frequently not under the original researcher's control and fixed for a given study) and features of the research methodology (frequently more under the original researcher's control and often variable within the study leading to multiple results). Uncontrollable or fixed features of a research environment must generally be taken as given and limit a piece of work to providing a single observation—for instance, data on a durable product such as a car may provide no direct evidence about packaged goods or pharmaceuticals. For this reason, it is desirable to study multiple products so that generalization about research environment is possible. By contrast, controllable characteristics may be varied within a study, which allows a given study to provide multiple pieces of evidence for a meta-analysis. For instance, alternative models can be fit to the same data, or the same model can be fit using alternative estimation procedures. Some examples of these features are as follows:

Fixed or Uncontrollable by Original Researcher	*Variable or Controllable by Original Researcher*

Product
  Durable
  Nondurable
  Industrial
  Service
	Model specification
	  Inclusion of exogenous or other
	  endogenous variables
	  Inclusion of carryover effects
	  Inclusion of time-varying parameters

Cultural environment	Functional specification
	  Inclusion of interactions
	  Inclusion of mean or slope shifts

Data measurement interval	

Nature of data
  Time series or cross-section
  Controlled experiment, natural
  experiment, or survey
	Estimation procedures
	  Crosstables versus multivariate
	  procedure
	  Single equation versus multiple
	  equation models
	  Linear versus nonlinear
	  measurement

Level of aggregation
  Brand versus market
  Aggregate versus individual
  promotional measurement	

Background discipline of the researcher	Measurement devices used
	  Nature of scales
	  Nature of experimental stimuli

Idiosyncratic characteristics of the sampling plan	Data collection method
	  Personal interview, diary, mail
	  questionnaire, scanner, telephone
	  interview
	  Panel or single wave

Type of respondent	Variable definitions
	  Share versus volume
	  Relative versus absolute price,
	  advertising

Even this classification of controllable and uncontrollable is somewhat imperfect. For example, the researcher may in fact have no control over the data collection method, which may be fixed before his or her involvement with the study. Similarly, the data interval may be partially under the researcher's control if the researcher is dealing with raw diary panel, store audit, or scanner data where the period of aggregation can be varied.

It is certain, however, that the process that produces a set of studies in an area will not produce a classic experimental design. Meta-analysis must look at a given study in the framework of a natural or accidental experiment. The remainder of this chapter discusses the construction of the underlying design used in the four studies described in chapter 2. The next chapter discusses methods for empirical analysis of these natural experimental designs.

The Fishbein Studies: Near Comparability

Despite an unusual degree of consistency in theory and method, differences across individual Fishbein studies allow them to be viewed as imperfect replications that use the same model in different situations and using different measurement methods. Five differences in situation and method were identified that might influence the parameters. These interstudy differences provide a basis for grouping studies and hence as classification suitable for an ANOVA:

1. The form of the attitudinal variable: A_{act} measured directly or $\Sigma B_i a_i$

2. The form of the normative variable: SN measured directly or $\Sigma NB_j MC_j$ Recently, $\Sigma B_i a_i$ and $\Sigma NB_j MC_j$ have been proposed (Fishbein and Ajzen 1975; Ryan and Bonfield 1975) as antecedents to A_{act} and SN, respectively. If this is so, A_{act} and SN should be stronger predictors of B_i than $\Sigma B_i a_i$ and $\Sigma NB_j MC_j$.

3. The method of inquiry: Survey versus experiment. There is an inherent trade-off in emphasizing internal or external validity (Runkel and McGrath 1972). The tight controls utilized in an experiment should lead to better model fit than that obtained in a survey setting.

4. The researchers' predominant discipline affiliation: Marketing or social psychology. Accepted sins of omission and commission vary across disciplines in regard to research standards. Psychologists, for example, have a long history of concern for measurement issues that has only recently emerged in marketing research (Ray 1979). Greater concern with measurement issues may reduce the random error in the model, thereby increasing obtained fits.

5. The type of subjects employed, either students or "real world" respondents. The use of student samples has long been debated (Alpert 1967; Sheth 1970; Ferber 1977). Since student samples are often convenient, it would be helpful to show that students react as a broader population does in these experimental situations.

The experimental design thus contains only five binary conditions—a comparatively small number of natural design variables. Further, the design variables are probably not equally important; for example, measurement issues are probably more important than researcher background.

The Advertising Studies: A Complex Natural Design

Compared to the Fishbein studies, there are a large number of potentially important differences in the 128 advertising models. In fact, simply identifying these differences and developing hypotheses about them is a major undertaking.

Differences Related to Model Specification, Measurement, and Estimation

Choice of specification and estimation techniques is generally under control of the researcher, and various alternatives are likely to be tried before a best version is chosen for publication.

Specification. Actual model specifications differ in terms of the variables included, the assumed timing of the advertising effect (especially in terms of carry-over of the impact of current advertising into the future), and the functional form of the equation used.

Variables Included. Specification bias may be caused by omission of variables correlated with those included in the equation, with the estimated advertising elasticities being biased in the direction of the relation between an omitted variable and sales. Because multicollinearity among the explanatory variables frequently is mentioned in the studies, it is unreasonable to assume that this bias does not exist. Also, a model misspecified by exclusion of important variables should not fit as well as one incorporating those variables unless the excluded variables are very highly correlated with those included in the models.

Carryover Effect. Clarke (1976) provides an in-depth examination of carryover coefficients in a set of studies similar to those we discuss. When omission of a carryover effect constitutes misspecification, upward bias of the coefficient for the current advertising will result if current and past advertising are correlated positively and if past advertising has a positive impact on current sales.

Functional Form.   The choice of an additive or multiplicative model can affect elasticity. In most multiplicative models, the short-term elasticity is constrained to be constant over the range of the demand function, whereas in linear models, the corresponding elasticity varies.

Variable Definition: Share versus Volume.   Dependent and advertising variables are measured in terms of both volume and share in the 128 models. Those specifications using sales volume as the dependent variable imply two effects for advertising: sales gained from a competitor and sales gained from a possible expansion of the market due to advertising. Use of market share as the dependent variable puts the impact of advertising on primary demand in both numerator and denominator, eliminating market expansion from consideration. Similarly, the use of advertising share implicitly assumes no impact of advertising volume per se. As a result, share elasticities may be smaller on average than elasticities computed on the basis of volume measurements.

Estimation Method.   There is ambiguity about how estimation method might affect estimated parameters. Advertising elasticities estimated with OLS (in contrast to simultaneous equations or multistep estimation procedures designed to address serial correlations in residuals or correlations of residuals and explanatory variables) are biased in the direction of the relationship of current advertising with current sales—a relationship generally expected to be positive. Because OLS procedures minimize squared error, models estimated with this method should fit better, other factors being equal.

Differences in Advertising Effects Related to the Research Environment

Even for a correctly specified model with appropriately estimated parameters, qualitative features of market environments might affect results. Unlike specification and estimation, these are usually not under the researcher's control.

Products.   There is no reason to expect that advertising response will vary among products, but there is reason to anticipate that it will vary according to information needs related to particular products and to the state of development of particular markets.

Product Types and Information Needs.   For experience goods (Nelson 1974), which are predominantly frequently purchased and frequently used products, experience is the major source of information, and hence advertising elasticity may be relatively low, other things being equal. For durables and new products, a search for sources of information (including advertising) is more likely to accompany purchase. For very expensive and high-risk purchases, however, the buyer tends to rely more on other types of communication, and advertising may be relatively less effective.

Product Life Cycle. Elasticities should be higher during the early growth phase, when a significant number of new customers are brought in as triers, than during the maturity phase of the product life cycle, when most customers have substantial experience.

National Setting. Although some evidence suggests that ratios of advertising to sales of individual products do not differ among countries (Leff and Farley 1980), differences in preferences, restrictions on advertising, and production cost structures may cause advertising elasticities to differ among geographic markets.

Level: Brand versus Product. A given advertising elasticity should be smaller at the brand level than at the product level when volume data are used, because at the product level advertising might affect total sales as well as sales gained at the expense of other brands.

Data Interval. Mounting evidence indicates that the measurement interval has a significant impact on coefficients of econometric models involving advertising (Bass and Leone 1983; Vanhonacker 1982), largely because of problems in matching time frame of advertising measurement and advertising effect on sales.

Time Series versus Cross-Sections. Regressions used to fit models to time-series data often cannot distinguish between lagged advertising effects and positive serial correlation in disturbances (Clarke and McCann 1973; Houston and Weiss 1974; Maddala and Vogel 1969). Because cross-sectional data are not subject to estimation problems caused by serial correlation in residuals, advertising elasticities estimated with time-series data should be smaller. Further, cross-sectional analysis captures level effects rather than dynamics, again suggesting that time-series elasticities may be smaller.

Media Definitions. Specific media measurements might produce either higher or lower elasticities than those shown by aggregate measurement, which combines media of different effectiveness.

The Buyer Behavior Models: Pooling Elasticities

Because of the relatively small sample sizes, meta-analysis of the four buyer behavior models requires pooling of elasticities involving all five endogenous variables into a single analysis. Since each endogenous variable enters into the system as both a dependent and an explanatory variable, the experimental design must take account of both roles. Although the pooling requires strong assumptions, it allows testing of whether the various elasticities vary systematically in concert with either the dependent or independent variable involved. The pooling also allows examination of some system properties.

The null hypothesis is that each variable affects each other to which it is linked equally. This is somewhat similar to assuming that all variables are measures of a single construct and, hence, that their intercorrelations should be equal.

Interstudy Differences

Differences across studies might also affect results. Because of the small number of studies, these may also nest within certain characteristics of model specifications as well. Among interstudy differences are the following:

Type of product (durable versus nondurable). The four products compare a durable and three nondurables. This breakdown, however, may obscure some interproduct differences.

Location of study. Studies were conducted in the United States, Argentina, and Kenya.

Parameter estimation. Ordinary least squares and two-stage least squares were used for estimation.

Measurement wave. Three of the studies use multiwave measurement, which may produce a panel effect (Sudman 1964).

Interview method. Personal and telephone interviewing was used.

Effects of various field procedures on measurements such as those used here (Payne 1974; Mayer 1974) might also affect relationships among these measurements (Farley et al. 1979).

Interactions

As in the other sets of studies, it is not possible to assess the impact of all interactions in a classic factorial design framework. Even if an identical set of elasticities were available from each study and the studies were configured as is required by a formal factorial design, the actual set of study characteristics implies the need for replication of outputs under 96 conditions (3 countries × 2 product types × 4 wave configurations × 2 parameter estimation procedures × 2 methods of interviewing)—far from the data now available. Analysis must thus concentrate on direct effects and on a subset of interactions suggested as important by theory or prior results.

In this case, theory points to interactions that might be important. The pairwise interactions of endogenous variables play a central role in the underlying theory of consumer behavior upon which the models were based (Howard and Sheth 1969), so including these interactions in the experimental design can be viewed as a way to assess the basic core relations among endogenous measures within the consumer behavior model. Unfortunately, it is not feasible to analyze many of the higher-order interactions or interactions involving exogenous variables because of limited degrees of freedom.

Certain direct effects in imperfect replications may in fact be interactions because of specification patterns in the underlying models. In this case, for example, the direct effects of two key controllable exogenous variables—price and distribution—are in fact interaction variables because they are specified only to effect purchase or intention in the four studies.

The basic approach to constructing the natural experimental designs for meta-analysis is to identify potentially salient differences in the studies and to indicate these with a set of dummy variables (1 if the particular study has that particular characteristic and zero otherwise). The whole set of dummy variables then becomes the basis for constructing the experimental design. What follow are examples of how the design was constructed for the four studies.

Incorporating Meta-Analytical Variables into a Model

Differences over brands, interviewing waves (time tracking under different marketing conditions), and interviewing groups constitute a basis for meta-analytic comparison of results from the car buyer behavior model.

Five waves of panel interviews with the person who would be the principal user of the new car were collected by telephone over an eighteen-month period: one wave prior to the introductory advertising campaign, two during the campaign, and two after the actual introduction of the new brand. Eight brands were studied.

Because the questionnaires contained many questions about each of the eight brands, it was not feasible to ask each respondent about each brand. The sample, which numbered 1,673 on the first wave (of which 709 remained on the fifth wave), was therefore split into four groups with each group asked about three of the brands, as follows: group 1: brands A and B, plus new brand; group 2: brands A and C, plus new brand; group 3: brands D and E, plus new brand; and group 4: brands F and G, plus new brand.

The basic car buyer behavior model described in figure 2–2 can be reformulated to incorporate meta-analysis directly into the structure (Farley et al. 1982). Of course, model reformulation generally means that the model must be refit to raw data as described in the next chapter. The reformulation here involves two elements. First, we add a lagged value of the endogenous dependent variable to each equation as an exogenous variable to estimate carryover effects in the endogenous variables. Second, we add variables to test for differences over time in coefficients of endogenous or exogenous variables and for differences in coefficient values among salient subgroups of the population—that is, a set of meta-analytical design variables is incorporated directly into the model.

The reformulated attitude equation for the Vega sample (which has four subgroups of respondents and four waves of data) is shown in equation 3.1:

$$y_{2t} = \beta_{24} y_{4t}$$

endogenous contemporaneous effects from original model (3.1a)

$$+ \gamma_{20} + \sum_{j=2}^{6} \gamma_{2j} x_j$$

exogenous variables from original model (3.1b)

$$+ \gamma_{2,10} y_{2,t-1}$$

carryover effects of lagged endogenous variable treated as exogenous (3.1c)

$$+ \left[\sum_{i=1}^{3} \alpha_{2i} G_i + \sum_{i=1}^{3} \delta_{2i} W_i \right]$$

group and time dummy variables allowing for differences in mean value of endogenous variables over groups and over time (3.1d)

$$+ \left[\sum_{i=1}^{3} \theta_{2i}(G_i \, y_{4t}) + \sum_{i=1}^{3} \psi_{2i}(W_i \, y_{4t}) \right]$$

interaction variables allowing for differences in slopes of endogenous variables over groups and over time (3.1e)

$$+ \left[\sum_{i=1}^{3} \sum_{j=2}^{6} \theta_{2ij}(G_i x_{ij}) \right.$$

interaction variables allowing for differences in slopes of exogenous variables over groups and over time (3.1f)

$$+ \left. \sum_{i=1}^{3} \sum_{j=2}^{6} \psi_{2ij}(W_i x_{ij}) \right]$$

$$+ u_{2t}$$

error term from original model (3.1g)

The approach incorporates tests for mean stability (Farley and Hinich 1970) and slope stability (Farley, Hinich, and McGuire 1975) of general regression models. The corresponding equation for the Volkswagen model differs from equation 2.2a in the fact that there are only two groups and hence fewer group parameters in equation 3.1d through 3.1f. Because of this, it is necessary to fit the model to the two brands separately, although all waves and available groups are used simultaneously for each brand. The variables in 3.1d, 3.1e, and 3.1f are the meta-analytic elements that add explanatory variables to each equation. The first variable, W_i, is a dummy variable that identifies the wave the observation comes from; the second, G_i, is a dummy that designates the sample subgroup to which an observation belongs. These variables will account for differences in means over time and over groups. The other variables are interaction terms containing 0s in the same positions as the zeros in the corresponding dummy variable but containing the value of an endogenous or exogenous variable in the positions in which the corresponding dummy variable contains a 1.

The two meta-analytic design elements incorporated directly into the model are thus:

1. Shifts in means and slopes of endogenous variables. Means shifting over time may indicate changes in the nature of the consumer decision-making process over the course of the introduction of a new brand. For example, increasing experience accompanying development of attitudes may precede a change in the impact of advertising on choice (Parsons 1976).

2. Intergroup differences. Identifiable subgroups exist within virtually any population. Even if respondents are assigned randomly to groups, there may still be differences in endogenous variables because of differences due to changes in such factors as different intergroup attrition rates. Intergroup differences in response may also be appropriate bases for definition of market segments (Claycamp and Massy 1968; Frank, Massy, and Wind 1975; Weinstein and Farley 1974).

Acceptance of the null hypothesis of a value of 0 for a given α or θ indicates that the corresponding mean or slope does not differ over sample groups. Acceptance of the hypothesis of 0 value for a given δ or ψ implies that the corresponding mean or slope does not vary over time.

Discussion

Identifying potentially salient differences over studies is not an extraordinarily difficult task, although a thorough familiarity with the underlying literature is necessary. Although it is always possible that an important factor is missed, this problem appears less crucial than difficulties associated with sorting out the impact of factors that are correlated.

The differences over studies do not in any way constitute an orderly method for assessment of these dimensions; that is, the design is quite accidental. These interstudy differences, however, do allow analysis of method differences that could not be assessed in the context of exact replication.

In practice, there is no necessary relationship between the complexity of the dependent variable and the complexity of the design, which are determined by different forces—the dependent variables mainly by the research tradition and the independent variables mainly by the research environment.

Insofar as significant differences over studies in results are not associated with these interstudy differences, generalizability of the studies as a whole is indicated. Insofar as the interstudy differences are associated with significant differences in results, conditional generalization is still possible, although this usually requires adjustment of the types described in the next chapter.

We are now ready to turn to empirical stages of meta-analysis, which proceed in two steps. The first step, discussed in chapter 4, is analysis of the natural experimental design. The second step involves the meta-analysis itself, which is discussed in chapter 5.

4

Analyzing the "Natural" Experimental Design

All meta-analysis goes through the steps of identifying the dependent variable and identifying salient differences over studies in the sample. Many meta-analyses, however, neglect what we consider one of the most important parts of the procedure: a careful assessment of the natural experimental design, leading to the construction of the statistical model for the meta-analysis itself.

On the rare occasions when raw data are available, we can incorporate the meta-analysis directly into estimation of the structural model, estimating both model parameters and meta-analytic parameters into the same step. Such a situation often allows us to avoid the problems discussed in this chapter. An example is discussed in chapter 5.

Most meta-analyses, however, are performed on summary statistics. In this case, there are two kinds of models involved: the models in the original studies, which provide the data for the meta-analysis, and a second statistical model, usually some sort of analysis of variance model, for the meta-analysis itself. The ANOVA model in the meta-analysis is usually quite different from the models used in the studies that provide the data base for the meta-analysis. In the case of the Fishbein meta-analysis, for example, the original model providing the inputs is of the form:

$$BI = \omega_1 A + \omega_2 SN, \tag{4.1}$$

while the meta-analysis model is a multivariate analysis of variance

$$X = u + \sum_{i=1}^{k} C_i Z_i + \epsilon \tag{4.2}$$

where X is a vector of outputs from 4.1 (ω_1, ω_2, and R), u is a vector of grand means, the C_i's are parameters for the design variables, the Z_i's the design variables in an $n \times k$ design matrix, and ϵ is a vector of errors. Analysis of the properties of the design matrices is the focus of this chapter.

Creating the data set for the meta-analysis is simple in principle. It requires filling in a table with data from the existing studies. Practically, this turns out to be both tedious and frustrating since the studies rarely report all the information needed, much less in a concise and easily identifiable fashion. Thus issues about units of measurement, what the model precisely contains, and other problems absorb a substantial amount of time. Often guesses will have to be made to complete the data set.

It is usually most convenient to code the design variables, which are categorical in nature, as dummy variables in preparation for use in a regression program. In general, using effects coding in the manner suggested by Draper and Smith (1966, pp. 244–262) is desirable, so the estimated ANOVA coefficients for a given effects sum to zero. This allows for easy testing of the maintained model of no differences over the variables. The recoding involves leaving out one dummy variable for each effect and coding the rest of the remaining dummies as −1 when the omitted variable equals one. It is most convenient to eliminate the dummy whose category mean is closest to the grand mean, and this will tend to be the category with the largest sample size. The recoded design variables center the entire analysis around the grand mean of the ANOVA. These dummy variables, along with any covariates that are included (such as continuous variables such as sample size), form the design matrix for the actual meta-analysis. On occasion, the effects coding itself injects an increased degree of collinearity into the estimation process, so it may be desirable to use simple one-zero dummy variables. However, since the ANOVA coefficients do not then sum to zero over an experimental effect, statistical testing of the coefficients is made more complicated. In rare cases, the natural experiment falls into a simple design like equation 4.2, for which analysis can use a specialized ANOVA or MANOVA program.

In practice, analysis of the natural experimental design involves dealing with three types of problems:

1. Inadequate effective sample size. It is usually possible to estimate only main effects and a few carefully prespecified interactions because the number of potential design variables is large relative to sample sizes available.

2. No or little variance in some design variables. The natural design is often severely imbalanced. For example, there may be many studies available from the United States but only one from South America. In practice, we have found that a design variable must be +1 for at least 10 percent of the sample (or equivalently less than 90 percent) to allow for reasonable stability in the estimation of its associated coefficient.

3. Confounding. The available observations often tend to be clustered in a few combinations of design variables, which means that the design variables are dependent as a set. As a result, it is difficult to decide unambiguously which design variable has an effect on the dependent variable. In other words, there is usually collinearity among the design variables. In the extreme, this collinearity may make inverting cross-products of the design matrix either impossible (due to perfect singularity) or difficult and unreliable, leading to large variances for the parameter estimates.

To deal with these problems, analysis of the experimental design—that is, of the recoded dummy variables—normally passes through four stages:

1. Eliminating absolutely redundant elements from the design.
2. Eliminating low variance design variables, usually by creating meaningful "all other" categories in the experimental design.
3. Specifying an ANOVA model involving main effects and a limited number of one-way interactions based on the literature or on theory.
4. Reducing or calibrating collinearity among the design variables.

The first three steps are relatively straightforward. The fourth step typically requires some careful thought and a choice between selecting only some representative variables (and accepting the attendant omitted variable bias) or creating indexes (for example, factor scores) that are independent but may not provide good insight. This chapter proceeds by first describing the process of meta-analysis in the context of a factorial design (an easy task) followed by specific examples of the adjustments required in meta-analyses in the studies described in this book.

The Meta-Analytic Ideal: Natural Factorial Design

Most meta-analyses do not explicitly recognize that there is an underlying ideal natural experimental design—the factorial design. A factorial design, with appropriate replication, allows assessment of all main effects plus interactions of all orders using orthogonal statistical tests that are relatively easy to construct. Should nature present the meta-analyst with a set of studies configured in a factorial design, life is quite easy.

In situations where the researcher is sure that interactions do not exist, a simpler experimental design involving only main effects is appropriate, but then only because the interactions in the factorial design are, in effect, constrained to be zero. Interactions can seldom be dismissed in meta-analysis in such a cavalier fashion, so the full factorial design is usually the best conceptual starting point.

Unfortunately, the natural processes that produce the actual studies available for a meta-analysis do not take heed of the optimality offered by the ideal factorial design. Effects and combinations of effects are always missing in the natural experimental design, and the realities of meta-analysis are frequently dominated by defects in the experimental design.

The underlying problem resulting from departure from factorial design is that the design variables in the natural experiment are correlated. As a result, a careful empirical assessment of the natural experimental design must be made. Definitional redundancies must first be removed. Since the cross-product of the matrix containing the design variables must generally be inverted at the next step of the meta-analysis, this matrix must be checked for full rank.

It is almost certain that the cross-product of the design matrix is not diagonal (for example, that the underlying natural experiment is not orthogonal), so the overall explanatory power of the meta-analysis will be larger than explanatory power that can be unambiguously imputed to the various factors in the design. The reason is that two or more factors will often have shared (confounded) explanatory power. In a factorial design, such shared explained variance is explicitly captured in the interaction terms. In most actual applications, however, the meta-analyst must adopt some reasonable way of dealing with shared variance. The problem of shared variance is so important in meta-analysis that it is a preoccupation of this chapter. In addition, chapter 6 is devoted to some relatively novel ways to deal with shared variance.

The Natural Design in the Fishbein Studies: Factorial Census in a Simple Situation

The natural experimental design in the case of the Fishbein studies is small enough that enumeration of the cases and comparison to a full factorial design is feasible.

The five systematic differences among studies discussed in chapter 3 (two types of measurement, experiment versus survey, researcher background, and type of sample) are dichotomous, so differences in the three parameters from each study might be analyzed with a 2^5 factorial multivariate analysis of variance (Bock 1975). It is obvious, however, that the available thirty-seven observations cannot fill each of the thirty-two cells with the full replication necessary for a simple orthogonal analysis of all interactions in the full factorial design. Further, the occurrence of observations in particular cells was not the result of an experimental design. On examination, the natural experiment in fact turns out to be highly imbalanced; sixteen of the thirty-two cells in a full factorial design are in fact empty, and nine more cells contain only one observation. The primary cause for the empty cells is that researchers used either direct measurements of both A and SN or else used the summated form for both but seldom mixed the two forms of measurement. The other twenty-eight observations are multiply located in the remaining seven cells of the factorial design. Thus, even in this nearly ideal setting, the meta-analysis must proceed in steps, starting with assessing main effects and then proceeding to assess interactions associated with significant main effects.

This imbalance immediately suggests a major implication of meta-analysis. In the future, it would be useful for each new application of a model to consider the role that it might play in filling in the quasi-experimental design. For example, is a new piece of work a replication of a cell that already has multiple entries, is it a replication of a single-entry cell, or is it the first entry in an experimental cell heretofore empty? Contribution of new work is greater if it fills an empty cell in the natural factorial design rather than replicating in a cell that already contains several observations. In the case of Fishbein models, for example, models that mix the summated and direct measurement of A and SN would be very useful. This view contrasts sharply with the periodic calls for replication and the attendant complaints about noncomparability that often appear in the journals. Exact replications are, of course, useful for judging reliability of results, but they have a special role to play that may be less important than that often imputed to them.

The Natural Experimental Design in the Advertising Studies: Problems of Imbalance and Complexity

The larger are the number of possibly salient differences over studies, the larger is the natural experimental design and the more difficult it is to develop a reasonable analysis plan. The nature of this problem is shown in table 4–1 where counts of the various types of differences in the econometric advertising studies discussed in chapter 3 are shown, summarized by the number of observations in each level of each of the 13 design variables. Although the 128 studies provided enough degrees of freedom to assess all 48 main effects (the sum of the numbers of levels shown for the categories in table 4–1), a full factorial experiment implies approximately 7 million cells (the product of the number of levels across the categories). Even the experimental design using only variables with 10 percent of the sample, probably the minimum for reasonable inference, contains about 140,000 cells. The data needed for analysis of all main effects and even a substantial fraction of interactions thus greatly exceed the relatively small number of available observations.

Table 4–1 also shows that the design is highly imbalanced and that it is dominated by studies of relatively mature products (109 of 128 studies) in the United States (105 of 128), incorporating carryover effects in the model formally (114 of 128). In practice, this high degree of imbalance has often made it difficult to analyze relatively rare situations in the natural design. In table 4–1, for example, 18 of 48 individual effects are represented in less than 10 percent of the sample.

As an empirical matter, a natural quasi-experiment will not have orthogonal factors, one of the major benefits of formal experimental design. When nonorthogonal factors are present, statistical testing of individual effects must address the problem of shared variance which is common to two or more effects. A feeling for the nature of this problem is shown in principal components analysis of the design variables in table 4–1 which are shown in table 4–2. In comparison with the ideal orthogonal experimental design for which all the eigenvalues are equal, the design using all the variables clearly involves almost insurmountable collinearity problems. Some relief is given by combining into "all other" classes those variables that occurred for less than 10 percent of the sample. Although some possibly interesting design factors are excluded when this is done, the short-term elasticities design appears to meet minimal conditions for inversion of

Table 4–1
Characteristics of 128 Advertising Studies and Univariate Tests on Within-Group Means of Studies with Those Characteristics

Descriptors of Model Specification and Estimation	Number of Studies	Short-term Elasticities	Carryover	Goodness of Fit
Model configuration				
Variables included (5 levels)				
Exogenous variables	74		−	
Price	72	+	−	−
Other marketing variables	23		−	
Product quality	7	×	×	×
Distribution	4	×	×	×
Pattern of timing (2 levels)				
Carryover in advertising effect	114	−	+	+
Time-varying advertising effect	12	×	×	×
Functional form (2 levels)				
Multiplicative	72	−		−
Additive	56	+		+
Variable definition				
Dependent variable (3 levels)				
Share	65	−	+	+
Volume	60	+		
Per capita	3	×	×	×
Advertising variable (3 levels)				
Share	40			
Volume	72	+	−	
Per capita	16	−	+	
Estimation methods (4 levels)				
Ordinary least squares	46			+
Nonlinear single equations	46	+	+	−
Multiple step single equations	28	−		
Multiple equations	8	×	×	×

Table 4–1 continued

Descriptors of Measurement and the Research Environment	Number of Studies	Short-term Elasticities	Carryover	Goodness of Fit
Product				
Product type (9 levels)				
Frequently purchased	71		+	
Food	26	−		−
Durables	20	+		−
Other nondurables	17		+	+
Detergents and cleaners	11	×	×	×
Pharmaceuticals and toiletries	10	×	×	×
Gasoline	7	×	×	×
Cigarettes	4	×	×	×
Lydia Pinkham	3	×	×	×
Position in life cycle (4 levels)				
Introductory	10	×	×	×
Growth	5	×	×	×
Maturity	109			
Decline	4	×	×	×
National setting (3 levels)				
United States	105	−		+
Europe	14	+		−
Elsewhere	9	×	×	×
Level (2 levels)				
Brand	86	−		−
Product	42	+		+
Data interval (3 levels)				
Monthly and weekly	41			
Bimonthly and quarterly	32	−	+	
Yearly	55	+	−	+
Data include cross-sections (2 levels)				
Yes	38		+	+
No	90			
Media definitions (6 levels)				
Aggregate	90	+		
Television	24	−		
Journals	4	×	×	×
Direct mail	4	×	×	×
Retail	4	×	×	×
Sampling and promotion	2	×	×	×

Source: Reprinted with permission from Gert Assmus, John U. Farley, and Donald R. Lehmann, "How Advertising Affects Sales: A Meta-Analysis of Econometric Results," *Journal of Marketing Research*, 21, no. 1 (February 1984), published by the American Marketing Association.

Note: + or − indicates sign of significant univariate test at $\alpha = .05$. × indicates sample too small to allow testing or inclusion in ANOVAS. In some cases these are grouped into an "all other" category for binary comparison.

the cross-product of the design matrix. However, the designs for the carry-over coefficients and goodness-of-fit measurements still have severe problems. (The matrices are different because of different available sample sizes for each of the

Table 4-2
Impact of Design Imperfections in Natural Experiment for 128 Advertising Studies

	All Design Variables from Table 4-1	Design Variables with Nonzero Values for at Least 10 Percent of Sample		
		Dependent Variables		
		Short-Term Elasticity	Carryover	Goodness of Fit
Principal components analysis of experimental design matrix				
Number of nonzero observations	128	128	114	109
Number of nonredundant variables	42	25	24	25
Ratio of largest to smallest eigenvalue	45,236	663	1800	1555
Determinant	6×10^{-20}	$.29 \times 10^{-12}$	$.58 \times 10^{-15}$	$.1 \times 10^{-15}$

Source: Reprinted with permission from Gert Assmus, John U. Farley, and Donald R. Lehmann, "How Advertising Affects Sales: A Meta-Analysis of Econometric Results," *Journal of Marketing Research*, 21, no. 1 (February 1984) published by the American Marketing Association.

dependent measures.) Several approaches are available for allocating shared explanatory power among factors and for estimating the effects of groups of variables (Green, Carroll, and DeSarbo 1978), but we do not use them because our main goal is to assess the impact of individual factors (for example, to estimate the significant ANOVA coefficients). The impact of the shared variance on the meta-analysis itself is discussed in the next chapter.

Design in the Buyer Behavior Studies: Singularity and the Need for Design Reduction

In many cases, the design itself must be reduced to make meta-analysis even feasible. This often occurs because of redundancies in the natural design—that is, because some factors are in effect the same. Although potentially interesting information may be lost, such reduction may be necessary, as it is in the case of the buyer behavior models.

The matrix form of the basic ANOVA model used in the meta-analysis of the buyer behavior studies is:

$$Y = X \quad \phi \quad + \quad \epsilon$$

Y	X	ϕ	ϵ
(113×1)	(113×56)	(56×1)	(113×1)
elasticities	design	ANOVA	errors
derived	matrix	parameters to	
from buyer		be estimated	
behavior		(including	
models		grand mean)	

The set of 55 explanatory variables plus the grand mean that are candidates for the ANOVA model is shown in table 4–3. All elements of the design matrix, X, are either 0 (the effect is absent) or 1 (the effect is present). The 56×56 matrix $(X'X)$ must be inverted to estimate the ANOVA parameters. Unfortunately, $(X'X)$ is not of the full rank required to estimate parameters. It is necessary to reduce the design variable set through a series of steps to achieve nonsingularity of $(X'X)$:

Step 1: Eliminating design variables with no variability. First, some variables in fact have no observations associated with them because the original structures of the buyer behavior models do not specify explicit relationships among all pairs of endogenous variables. Here, three of the twenty possible interaction (table 4–3) terms must be eliminated because they have zero variance, resulting in a reduced $(X'X)$ matrix, which is 53×53.

Table 4–3
Candidate Variables for ANOVA Model and Their Disposition in the Variable Reduction Process

Causal Variables						Endogenous System Variables		
Direct Effects of Dependent Variables	Variable Eliminated?	ANOVA Model Coefficient	Direct Effects of Endogenous Explanatory Variables	Variable Eliminated?	ANOVA Model Coefficient	Pairwise Interactions of Endogenous Dependent and Explanatory Variables	Variable Eliminated?	ANOVA Model Coefficient
Awareness[a]	Yes[a]	—	Awareness	Yes[a]	—	Awareness-Knowledge	Yes[a]	—
Knowledge	No	α_1	Knowledge	No	β_1	Awareness-Attitude	Yes[a]	—
Attitude	No	α_2	Attitude	No	β_2	Awareness-Purchase	Yes[a]	—
Purchase	No	α_3	Purchase	No	β_3	Awareness-Satisfaction	Yes[a]	—
Satisfaction	No	α_4	Satisfaction	No	β_4	Knowledge-Awareness	Yes[a]	—
						Knowledge-Attitude	Yes[c]	—
						Knowledge-Purchase	Yes[c]	—
						Knowledge-Satisfaction	Yes[c]	—
						Attitude-Awareness	Yes[a]	—
						Attitude-Knowledge	Yes[c]	—
						Attitude-Purchase	Yes[c]	—
						Attitude-Satisfaction	Yes[b]	—
						Purchase-Awareness	Yes[a]	—
						Purchase-Knowledge	Yes[c]	—
						Purchase-Attitude	No	γ_{32}
						Purchase-Satisfaction	No	γ_{34}
						Satisfaction-Awareness	Yes[a]	—
						Satisfaction-Knowledge	Yes[b]	—
						Satisfaction-Attitude	Yes[b]	—
						Satisfaction-Purchase	No	γ_{44}

Exogenous Variables

Exogenous Systems Variables

Controllable Exogenous Variables	Variable Eliminated?	ANOVA Model Coefficient	Noncontrollable Exogenous Variable	Variable Eliminated?	ANOVA Model Coefficient
Distribution	No	β_5	Past purchase	No	β_{10}
Price	No	β_6	Family income	No	β_{11}
Advertising measures			Age of head	No	β_{12}
Exposure			Family size	No	β_{13}
Radio	No	β_7	Interest in product	No	β_{14}
Print	No	β_8			
Television	Yes[c]	β_9			

Study Characteristics	Variable Eliminated?	ANOVA Model Coefficient
Country		
Kenya	Yes[c]	—
Argentina	No	δ_1
United States	Yes[a]	—
Product		
Durable	No	δ_2
Nondurable food	Yes[c]	—
Nondurable nonfood	Yes[a]	—
Wave in panel		
Wave 1	Yes[c]	—
Wave 2	No	δ_3
Wave 3	No	δ_4
Wave 4	Yes[a]	—
Method of parameter estimation		
Ordinary least squares	Yes[a]	—
Two-stage least squares	No	δ_5
Interviewing method		
Personal	No	δ_6
Telephone	Yes[a]	—

Source: Reprinted by permission from "Patterns in Parameters of Buyer Behavior Models: Generalizing from Sparse Replication," John U. Farley, Donald R. Lehmann, and Michael J. Ryan, *Marketing Science*, 1, no. 2 (Spring 1982) Copyright 1982, The Institute of Management Sciences, 290 Westminster Street, Providence, RI 02903.

[a] Variables selected for omission from each set to avoid redundancy in regression.
[b] Variables eliminated because no observations are available.
[c] Variables eliminated in step-wise regression.

Step 2: Eliminating definitional redundancy. Even this reduced matrix, however, is singular because of the redundancy of subsets of design variables and the constant term. For example, the coefficients of the dependent endogenous variables form such a set because each elasticity must have one of the five as the dependent variable. This problem is resolved by eliminating one variable from each such redundant set of direct effects, along with all interactions associated with these eliminated variables. The choice of variables to eliminate does not affect the results, provided that the remaining variables are coded to maintain the classical condition that complete subsets of the ANOVA coefficients sum to zero, for example

$$\sum_i \alpha_i = \sum_j \beta_j = \sum_i \sum_j \gamma_{ij} = 0.$$

Table 4–3 indicates the 15 variables chosen for elimination. After elimination of definitionally redundant variables (and replacement of zeros in corresponding positions of retained variables with −1 using the procedure in Draper and Smith 1966, pp. 243–262), the reduced $(X'X)$ matrix is 38×38.

Step 3: Eliminating empirical redundancy. Even this reduced matrix is empirically singular as it has only 33 nonzero characteristic roots.

Some further insight into this problem is gained by examination of two submatrices, one identifying 28 dependent and explanatory intrastudy variable pairings and the other identifying 10 variables summarizing interstudy characteristics. Not only is the overall design covariance matrix singular but so are both key submatrices:

	Overall Design Covariance Matrix	*Submatrix Identifying Within-Study Characteristics**	*Submatrix Identifying Interstudy Characteristics*
Dimensionality	38×38	28×28	10×10
Number of eigenvalues			
Greater than 1	16	9	3
From 0.1 to .99	15	15	5
Less than 0.1	2	1	0
Total greater than 0	33	24	8
Singular?	Yes	Yes	Yes

*Endogenous and exogenous variable pairings in a given elasticity

It is clear that further reduction of the design matrix is needed in order to have a specified model with estimatable parameters, and this must be done empirically. It is desirable to avoid this empirical step if possible. One option is to replace raw values in the design matrix with values of principal components, with attendant loss in ability to make inferences about particular design elements. An information-retaining method is to use a step-wise regression procedure in the reduction, using elasticities as dependent variables and the remaining design elements as independent variables. This approach has the effect of loading the analysis in favor of finding significant effects (for example, nonzero values for the individual ANOVA coefficients) because partial association with the dependent variable is used as the criterion for inclusion of an explanatory variable. Since the maintained model is that there are no significant differences, this step makes the subsequent tests very stringent. Application of this stepwise approach to the 38 design elements led to retention of 27 variables in the design matrix, with the procedure stopping at the point that none of the remaining variables contributed as much as one-tenth of 1 percent of incremental explanatory power of the dependent variables.

Patterns in the design variables retained after these steps (table 4–4) indicate that the majority of direct effects survive the reduction. All endogenous direct effects (dependent and explanatory) are retained, as are all but one direct

Table 4–4
Variables Retained in Design Matrix after Step-Wise Regression

	Number of Variables Left in Design after Removal of Definitional Redundancies and Nonexisting Combinations	Number of Variables Retained after Step-Wise Regressions
Endogenous system variables		
Dependent endogenous variables	4	4
Explanatory endogenous variables	4	4
Interactions of endogenous variable pairings	9	3
Exogenous system variables		
Controllable	6	5
Noncontrollable	5	5
Study Characteristics	9	6
Total	37	27

Source: Reprinted by permission from "Patterns in Parameters of Buyer Behavior Models: Generalizing from Sparse Replication," John U. Farley, Donald R. Lehmann, and Michael J. Ryan, *Marketing Science*, 1, no. 2 (Spring 1982), Copyright 1982, The Institute of Management Sciences, 290 Westminster Street, Providence, RI 02903.

exogenous effect. Three interactions are included, and all of these have purchase as one of the two elements of the elasticity in question. Six of 9 study characteristics are also retained. Relative to the sample size of 113 observations, the final reduced working set of 27 variables is small enough for parameter estimation to be reasonable. A summary of the steps used to arrive at this working design matrix follows:

	Number of Variables in Explanatory Set (Excluding the Grand Mean)	Design Covariance Matrix Singular?
Original design variable set	55	Yes
Remaining variable set after elimination of variables with no variance	52	Yes
Remaining variable set after elimination of redundancy so ANOVA is feasible	38	Yes
Remaining variable set after elimination of variables contributing less than .001 partial explanation of each dependent variable	27	No

As is usually the case with a natural experiment, even this reduced design covariance matrix is still not diagonal. When the experimental design is not orthogonal, either within variable groupings or among the studies, it is generally more convenient to estimate parameters with a regression program than with a prestructured ANOVA procedure, although both will produce the same result. The nonorthogonality generally also means that shared variance remains a problem. Chapter 6 discusses a series of approaches for dealing with shared variance.

Discussion

In our experience, exploring the nature of the experimental design is the most tedious and time-consuming step in meta-analysis. It is also the step that requires the most creative thinking because there is no fixed way to go about it. It is unconventional in terms of standard statistical analysis. Univariate analysis, eliminating and combining rare elements, and sequential checking for rank of the cross-product of the design matrix require careful attention. This step also requires patience because it often appears to hold up progress on the meta-analysis itself. In return, many insights into the nature of what has been done in a field emerge. In addition, the process of examining the experimental design generally leads toward the appropriate method for the meta-analysis itself.

The major goal of the assessment of characteristics of the natural experimental design is to be sure that the design matrix, almost always nonorthogonal, is configured in such a way that its cross-product is of full rank and thus can be inverted. This always involves elimination of design variables with no variance (unobserved or universal experimental conditions) and definitional redundancies such as those that occur normally in analysis of variance. Experience has also shown that factors that occur rarely must also be eliminated because they produce unstable estimates. This is usually best done by combining rare events into larger classes of similar or related factors.

Assessment of the experimental design should also involve an assessment of the degree of imperfection of the experiment, probably done most effectively by inspection of the eigenvalues of the cross-products of the design matrix. If some of the eigenvalues are zero, the design must be further reduced either by judgment or by application of some sort of step-wise procedure, such as step-wise regression, to eliminate the least promising factors from the design. This step, although undesirable, is necessary for the analysis to proceed. If there is great discrepancy between the value of the eigenvalues (if the largest is 1,000 times the smallest, for example), shared variance is likely to be a problem even though the required inversion is possible in principle. Shared variance—the ANOVA analogue of collinearity—involves variability in the dependent variable which can be explained by combinations of design variables but cannot be attributed unambiguously to individual factors. Calibration of shared variance is an important outcome of meta-analysis since it helps measure how the experimental factors are interrelated.

5
The Meta-Analysis

Only after a set of related studies has been carefully collected and the dependent variables defined, an appropriate set of design variables identified, and the natural design examined in detail can the meta-analysis itself proceed. If these steps are not completed carefully, a great deal of extra work and reestimation is required. Once they are completed, the time has finally arrived to do the statistical work for the meta-analysis itself.

Meta-Analytic Null Hypothesis

The basic null hypothesis underlying the meta-analytic statistical model is that all estimated values of the dependent variables (made comparable by appropriate statistical adjustment if necessary)—the advertising elasticities, the parameters of the Fishbein model—are equal to a grand mean under the various design conditions discussed in chapters 3 and 4. In our Fishbein studies, for example, the null hypothesis is that ω_1 and ω_2 are equal in all studies and that all the models fit equally well. This null hypothesis is quite different from the more conventional null hypotheses, ordinarily that parameter values are zero, used in each of the individual studies assembled to do the meta-analysis. One corollary of meta-analysis is that the conventional zero-value null hypothesis underlying conventional statistical inference makes no sense after the history of a field of inquiry builds up a string of rejections of zero values for model parameters. In fact, researchers seem wedded to the null hypothesis of no effect in the face of overwhelming prior evidence of its falsity.

Statistical testing of the meta-analytical null hypotheses can use any statistical procedure, such as cross-tabulations, order statistics, and t-tests. However, some statistical realities of the natural designs discussed in chapter 4 tend to dictate methods of analysis.

Correlated Explanatory Factors.   Natural experimental designs do not in practice provide independent factors. As a result, multivariate procedures are generally required for meta-analysis. Since the dependent variables are generally metric and the design variables are in the main qualitative, meta-analysis is likely to use procedures in the general family of analysis of variance, including multivariate analysis of variance when the dependent variable contains multiple elements and analysis of covariance when the experimental design includes some metric elements.

Relatively Few Observations.   The small effective sample sizes, caused primarily by the combination of a large number of elements in the factorial design and highly imbalanced samples, have two major influences on choice of analytical method. The first is that cross-tabular methods, beyond perhaps simple 2 × 2 breakdowns, are not useful because of small within-cell sample sizes. Moreover, such simple cross-tabbing is often not particularly useful because of the correlation of explanatory factors.

The second result of the relatively small sample sizes is that degrees of statistical freedom are so limited that most analysis must focus on direct effects of individual variables and disregard all but a handful of prespecified interactions. That is, analysis must proceed by expanding a main effects model rather than by simplifying a factorial model through elimination of interactions.

This relative sparseness of the data makes meta-analysis in some ways similar to archaeology where a few important clues and some general notions are used to construct an admittedly incomplete understanding of a situation. The archaeologist would, of course, be pleased to be able to observe his subjects in real life directly and to interview and otherwise take measurements on them. This is in general impossible so archaeology must work with what clues are available.

Nonavailability of Raw Data.   Meta-analysis must in general utilize summary statistics because raw data are not usually available and would generally be difficult to pool over observations even if they were available. When inputs to the meta-analytical process are summary statistics, sample sizes are necessarily small. One benefit, however, is that the relatively strong assumptions about error structures underlying the meta-analytic statistical procedures are to some extent met. For example, the summary statistics themselves are usually estimated with the assumption that estimation error is normally distributed, and the averaging processes used in parameter estimation in the original models tend to produce normal errors in these parameters. However, heteroscedasticity remains a potential problem and should be investigated, particularly when parameters differ by an order of magnitude.

There are four basic types of meta-analysis.

1.   Meta-analysis across studies using summary statistics of study results. This

is the type we had in mind when we began working with meta-analysis, and on which we have concentrated our efforts. Examples are provided by our analyses of the Fishbein studies, the advertising effects studies, and the buyer behavior studies. Even this sort of approach often uses multiple observations from a single study.

2. Within-study meta-analysis of summary statistics from one study. Occasionally a single study provides sufficient summary data under enough different conditions to allow analysis across brands, across market segments, or across time. We demonstrate how a correlation matrix might be decomposed in order to understand the structure of the data based on the new car study.

3. Meta-analysis within-study based on raw data. When the raw data are available, it is possible to test directly for the equality of effects across various brands, time periods, or sampling groups. A varying parameter formulation combines the meta-analysis model with the structural model in which parameters are estimated. As an example, we examine model coefficients using the new car data.

4. Meta-analysis across studies based on raw data. The ideal situation for meta-analysis would involve appropriate pooling of raw data across a large number of comparable studies using variable parameter structures, in effect, combining types 2 and 3. Unfortunately it is hard to find a set of studies comparable enough so that pooling makes sense. Moreover, the likelihood of a large number of authors giving up (or even having available) raw data is relatively low. We know of no marketing examples of this type of meta-analysis.

Across-Study Meta-Analysis of Summary Statistics

There are several approaches to the multivariate analysis of summary statistics, most of which boil down to application of some sort of analysis of variance model.

Analysis When the Same Model Parameters Are Available
from All Studies: MANOVA on Fishbein Results

When several studies produce sets of the same parameters, meta-analysis can be structured as a multivariate analysis of variance. The three Fishbein model parameters—ω_1, ω_2, and $\overline{R}$—provide such an opportunity. As a first step, a nonorthogonal multivariate analysis of variance (MANOVA) was performed (Bock 1975) to test main effects. The nonorthogonality and imbalance of the design made it infeasible to incorporate the full set of interactions directly into the analysis, as was discussed in chapter 4. However, the problem is structured well enough to allow a standard MANOVA computer routine to be used in estimation.

Results. Of the five main effects, only the discipline of the researcher was significant (table 5–1). To probe this result, a series of four 2 × 2 factorial designs was performed that crossed the researcher's discipline with each of the four other main effects that had at least four observations in each cell. Of these, only the analysis crossing attitudinal form and the researcher's discipline produced significant effects (table 5–2). Social psychologists obtained a better fit (figure 5–1) with the $\Sigma B_i a_i$ attitude form than with the A_{act} form, whereas the opposite held for marketing researchers. In principle, A_{act} should consistently provide a better fit than $\Sigma B_i a_i$ if in fact $\Sigma B_i a_i$ is an antecedent to A_{act}. The method used to structure attitudinal questions may help explain the better fit obtained by social psychologists using the multiplicative form of attitude. Marketing researchers often use a list of attributes predetermined by prior research or manager's experience, while social psychologists more often elicit outcomes from the respondents before belief and evaluation statements are constructed (Ryan and Etzel 1976). As a result, social psychologists may be using more salient attributes

Table 5–1
Dependent Variable Means For Five Main Effects

Variable	$\overline{\omega}_1$	$\overline{\omega}_2$	R	N
Attitudinal form, $F(3,29) = 2.76, p \le 0.06$				
A_{act}	0.46	0.28	0.72	28
$\Sigma B_i a_i$	0.41	0.37	0.67	9
Normative form, $F(3,29) = 0.86, p \le 0.47$				
SN	0.45	0.25	0.72	13
$\Sigma NB_j MC_j$	0.45	0.33	0.71	24
Researcher discipline, $F(3,29) = 7.2, p \le 0.001$				
Social psychology	0.43	0.38	0.79	18
Marketing	0.47	0.23	0.64	19
Research method, $F(3,29) = 0.87, p \le 0.46$				
Experimental	0.46	0.35	0.73	13
Correlational	0.44	0.27	0.70	24
Type of sample, $F(3,29) = 0.41, p \le 0.74$				
Students	0.48	0.29	0.73	26
Real world	0.39	0.34	0.65	11

Source: Reprinted with permission from John U. Farley, Donald R. Lehmann, and Michael J. Ryan, "Generalizing from 'Imperfect' Replication," *Journal of Business*, 54, no. 4 (October 1981), The University of Chicago Press, © 1981 by the University of Chicago. All rights reserved.

Table 5–2

2 × 2 Factorial Dependent Variable Means, MANOVA, ANOVA, and
Standardized Discriminant Weights

	Means			
	$\overline{\omega}_1$	$\overline{\omega}_2$	$\overline{R}$	N
Interaction of discipline and attitudinal form				
Social psychology $\times$ A_{act}	0.41	0.36	0.77	14
Social psychology $\times$ $\Sigma B_i a_i$	0.48	0.43	0.83	4
Marketing $\times$ A_{act}	0.51	0.20	0.67	14
Marketing $\times$ $\Sigma B_i a_i$	0.35	0.32	0.53	5

Source: Reprinted with permission from John U. Farley, Donald R. Lehmann, and Michael J. Ryan, "Generalizing from 'Imperfect' Replication," *Journal of Business*, 54, no. 4 (October 1981), The University of Chicago Press, © 1981 by the University of Chicago. All rights reserved.

in attitude measurements. Unfortunately, a description of the methodology of how attributes were determined was missing for nineteen of the thirty-seven studies, so a formal test on this issue is not possible.

Discussion of the Fishbein ANOVA Results. In terms of overall patterns, the thirty-seven studies using the Fishbein model are nearly replicative in the sense that model parameters showed little systematic variation with the five main effects used in MANOVA. The magnitude of the only statistically significant effect of researcher discipline in the measures of goodness of fit was small.

The insignificant effect on model coefficients of four potentially major sources of variation (attitudinal form, normative form, research method, and type of sample) has useful implications. For example, the traditional concern that parameter estimates obtained with student samples do not represent the real world (Ferber 1977) does not appear to apply to the Fishbein results. Guidance may also be available for needs for future research that would not normally result from conventional qualitative literature review. For example, results on attitudinal form are nearly significant. Since the cells contain a disproportionate distribution of observations of the two approaches (nine versus twenty-eight), more work using the multiplicative attitudinal form may provide closure on this measurement-related issue. This work can be done by measuring attitude both ways and comparing the results within a given study.

Meta-analysis of the Fishbein literature involves nearly ideal conditions in terms of interstudy comparability of measurement methods, estimation procedures, and model structures. Slightly different results are obtained by researchers in different fields, especially in terms of goodness of fit, but we would predict average multiple correlations of future studies will be about 0.7 and that ω_1 will be larger than ω_2 (about 0.45 versus 0.3). These values would seem to constitute

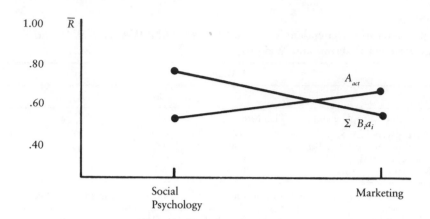

Figure 5–1. Means of $\overline{R}$ for Attitudinal Form × Researcher's Discipline Interaction

more useful null hypotheses at this point than would continued use of null hypotheses of zero for statistical testing.

Analysis When Sample Sizes Are Not Identical: Parallel ANOVAs

When sample sizes of various parameters are not the same because of reporting differences or different model structures, analysis is often best approached through a series of similarly structured analyses of variance. Such a situation occurs in the results from econometric advertising models. Although the parameters of the models appear to be the same (short-term advertising elasticity, carryover coefficient and coefficient of determination), not all parameters are available for all studies, producing different sample sizes. Further, eliminating the studies with missing parameters is undesirable because potentially interesting information is lost. For example, incorporating the studies without specified carryover effects allows testing of specification differences that would not be possible if those studies were eliminated.

As with the Fishbein studies, size and structure of the sample relative to the full factorial design make it impossible to do much with interactions. Further, results in chapter 4 indicated a high degree of imbalance and potential shared variability in the actual design.

Results.   Although the design is much more complex in this case than in any of our other examples, the results are potentially much richer. As is the case with much statistical analysis, it is useful to start simply to get some general feeling for the results. Using only those variables with at least ten observations to preserve minimal within-cell sample sizes, we performed univariate t-tests comparing mean values of estimates from studies with a given characteristic against all other estimates. Many more are significant than would be expected by chance:

	Number of Significant Differences		
Number of Tests	Short-term Elasticity	Carryover Coefficient	Goodness of Fit
29	20	13	15

These t-tests cannot be considered independent, but they do give some insight into the existence of identifiable patterns of difference across studies.

The ANOVA results, which are shown in table 5–3 contain the proportion of variance of each dependent variable explained by each factor in the natural experiment. Because of different sample sizes, a separate ANOVA was fit for each of the three dependent variables. Only those design variables represented in at least 10 percent of the sample are used here.

The proportion of variance uniquely attributable to each factor is calculated by subtracting the variance explained by all other factors from the variance explained by all the factors, thus creating an incremental value of variance unambiguously explained by that factor. In addition to isolating the unique variance explained by each factor, this also allows a simple assessment of the importance of shared variance by subtracting the sum of the incremental variability explained by each factor from the overall coefficient of determination of the ANOVA. As table 5–3 also indicates, the deficiencies in the natural experiment design cause significant sharing of explained variance among factors, especially for goodness of fit and carryover, for which the variable set as a whole has significant explanatory power but where shared variance dominates the results. It is important to recognize that calibration of shared variance is a result rather than a deficiency of meta-analysis. In fact, chapter 6 suggests some ways in which meta-analysis can use shared variance creatively.

Shared variance is a lesser problem for the short-term elasticities, for which seven ANOVA design variables are significant. Numerical values of the individual ANOVA coefficients for short-term elasticities significant in table 5–3 represent systematic effects in the results:

Grand Mean. The grand mean in the short-term elasticity ANOVA is 0.695, significantly greater than zero and also significantly greater than the arithmetic

Table 5–3
Fraction of Variability in Three Study Outputs Explained by Various
Study Characteristics

Study Characteristic	Degrees of Freedom	Dependent Variable		
		Short-Term Elasticity	Carryover Coefficient	Goodness of Fit
Model specification				
Variables included				
Exogenous variables	1	0.020*	0.021	0.002
Price	1	0.007	0.000	0.000
Other marketing variables	1	0.000	0.005	0.006
Advertising carryover included	1	0.094**	NA[a]	0.016
Functional form	1	0.037*	0.000	0.019
Variable definitions				
Dependent variable	1	0.018	0.008	0.009
Advertising variable	1	0.004	0.004	0.014
Measurement				
Data interval	2	0.035*	0.005	0.005
Pooled data	1	0.029*	0.008	0.051**
Media definitions	3	0.013	0.000	0.000
Estimation	3	0.026	0.001*	0.023*
Research environment				
Product type				
Frequently purchased	1	0.005	0.001	0.005
Food	1	0.034*	0.002	0.004
Other nondurables	1	0.000	0.002	0.020
Durables	1	0.006	0.000	0.023*
Mature product	1	0.004	0.000	0.012
National setting	2	0.027*	0.005	0.002
Brand or product	1	0.002	0.001	0.004
Variance explained by corresponding ANOVA				
Fraction of variability explained by individual variables		0.361**	0.073	0.215
Shared variance		0.140	0.526*	0.376**
Fraction of variability explained by ANOVA (R^2)		0.501**	0.599*	0.591*

Source: Reprinted with permission from Gert Assmus, John U. Farley, and Donald R. Lehmann,
"How Advertising Affects Sales: A Meta-Analysis of Econometric Results," *Journal of Marketing
Research*, 21, no. 1 (February 1984), published by the American Marketing Association.
[a]Not applicable. One design variable lost as all equations are specified to include a lagged dependent
variable.
*Significant at $\alpha = 0.05$.
**Significant at $\alpha = 0.01$.

mean of the elasticities. Advertising may be generally more effective in the short
term than the average estimated elasticities in table 2–3 suggest.

Carryover. The largest numerical effect is that short-term elasticities are 0.336

higher in models without a carryover coefficient than in models with one. The effect of an unspecified carryover is apparently picked up largely in the estimate of the short-term elasticity. The fact that models with and without a carryover term fit equally well also indicates that the larger short-term elasticity captures both effects when carryover is not specified.

Exogenous Variables Included.   Models containing exogenous variables have short-term elasticities 0.103 smaller than those of models lacking exogenous variables. Equations including exogenous variables also have estimated carryover coefficients 0.162 less than those of equations without them, indicating that longer-term elasticities may be overstated even more than short-term elasticities in models lacking exogenous variables. Because most exogenous variables commonly used in marketing models (income, family size, population, and others) are by hypothesis positively related to sales, their omission appears to overstate the effect of advertising.

Functional Form.   As predicted, elasticities in additive models are a significant 0.247 higher than elasticities estimated under the more restrictive multiplicative specification in which they are assumed equal over the range of data. The analytical convenience afforded by models linear in logarithms appears to lead to averaged-down estimated advertising elasticities.

Data Interval.   The increasing attention to the impact of a measurement period on estimated advertising effect is justified. Short-term elasticities based on various measurement periods differ relative to the grand mean as follows: weekly or monthly, −0.068; bimonthly or quarterly, 0.072; and annually, −0.004.

Type of Data.   As anticipated, pooled data (involving cross-sections) produced elasticities 0.176 larger than those of straight time-series data, suggesting that cross-sectional disaggregation of time series should be done whenever possible. Equations fit to pooled data also fit significantly better than those fit to straight time series.

Products.   Many studies do not provide explicit product identification, but food products (presumably from among the most heavily advertised in that category) have an elasticity 0.101 higher than that of the other categories. As expected, equations fit to data for durable goods fit significantly less well.

Locations.   Estimated short-term advertising elasticities for Europe are 0.039 greater than the grand mean but average 0.087 smaller than the grand mean for the United States. It appears that either Europeans underadvertise (perhaps because of media restrictions) or U.S. companies overadvertise for some unspecified reason.

Perhaps as important as the significant results are effects that are not significant. No significant differences in short-term elasticities are found in models using shares versus levels of sales or in models using brand versus products. This lack of significance may be related to the fact that the majority of products studied are relatively mature, so advertising has a relatively minor impact on product class sales. Also, there is not a significant effect of estimation method on short-term elasticities, although multiple-step single-equation methods produce significantly lower coefficients for the lagged dependent variables and multiple-equation methods produce significantly higher values. Finally, OLS produced better fits than other methods, as expected, since it minimizes squared error about the mean.

Discussion. In the future, tests of hypotheses for econometric advertising models should use null values for short-run advertising elasticities and lag effects other than zero. The mean values of the studies (short-term elasticity of about 0.3, carryover coefficient of about 0.5, and coefficients of determination of about 0.7) provide good initial estimates. These can be adjusted using the significant ANOVA coefficients. Models should also incorporate carryover structures and relevant controllable and uncontrollable exogenous variables; otherwise advertising effects are likely to be overstated.

Like the Fishbein results, the major implication for future research is that, in general, programmed research should be used to help remedy the defects of the natural experimental design. The univariate tests suggest that the impact of several factors related to significant differences in short-term and long-term advertising response coefficients, as well as how well models fit, may be obscured by a high degree of common or shared variance in the experimental design. New data are needed to expand available combinations of characteristics of the research environment—for example, more new products, more nonconsumer products, and new cultural settings. Other results can be filled out by experimentation with alternative specifications and estimation procedures on existing data. In addition to studies in other research settings, it would be useful to expand the available data base by surveying academic and industrial sources for models that have not been published, in many cases because of odd results, which might help fill in this highly nonorthogonal design.

Pooling Results When Data Are Sparse: Meta-Analysis of Buyer Behavior System Models

The elasticities derived from four buyer behavior models must be pooled into a single analysis structured as shown in table 4–3 in order to have an adequate sample size for analysis. An important part of the meta-analysis is thus to check the reasonableness of this pooling, which in effect says that all of the elasticities can be viewed as being generated by the same process. This does not mean that they are equal, but it does mean that differences in their values should occur in predictable patterns that can be calibrated by ANOVA.

The meta-analysis is structured as an ANOVA containing the variables remaining after the variable reduction process described in chapter 4 to make estimation feasible.

The ANOVA model used in the meta-analysis is for a given elasticity:

$$\eta_{ijkl} = u + \alpha_i + \beta_j + \gamma_{ij} + \sum_{s=1}^{t} \delta_{sk} + \epsilon_{ijk} \tag{5.1}$$

where η_{ijkl} is an elasticity computed from coefficients from a regression in which variable i is the dependent variable, variable j is the explanatory variable, the coefficient comes from a model with characteristics k, and from study 1; u is the grand mean; α_i is the incremental contribution of the endogenous dependent variable i to the elasticity; β_j is the incremental contribution of explanatory variable j, which may be either endogenous or exogenous, to the elasticity; γ_{ij} is the incremental contribution of the interaction of variables i and j, in those cases in which both are endogenous; δ_{sk} is the incremental effect of characteristic s in study k, which produced that elasticity (these effects, described in detail later, include product types, country, and various types of measurement and estimation methods); and ϵ_{ijk} is the error term of elasticity η_{ijkl}.

The pooling of the elasticities across models and variables in the ANOVA model allows testing of a set of hypotheses about the elasticities involving both individual variables and combinations of variables.

H_1: $u = 0$. Although the hypothesis about the value of the ANOVA grand mean is often substantively neutral, all elasticities in this case except those involving price are by hypothesis positive. Failure to reject this hypothesis will occur if all deviation of the elasticities from 0, except for the price effect, is traceable to specific variables and no core model structure exists among the endogenous variables.

H_2: $\alpha_i = 0$ $i = 1, \ldots, 5$. Acceptance of this hypothesis implies equality of elasticities for all dependent variables, other things equal.

H_3: $\beta_j = 0$ $j = 1, \ldots, 14$. Equality of elasticities over causal variables indicates the systems are equally responsive to changes in causal factors, both endogenous and exogenous. A priori this is not likely because the explanatory variables contain a mixture of endogenous variables ($\beta_j, j = 1, \ldots, 4$), which should have a fairly large impact on the system because of their central role in the theory, controllable exogenous variables ($\beta_j, j = 5, \ldots, 9$) such as price, advertising, and distribution, which should also have significant and immediate impact, and sociodemographic variables (β_j, $j = 10, \ldots, 14$), which have generally been shown to exert relatively small systematic impact on endogenous dependent variables in these systems (Farley and Sexton 1982; Weinstein and Farley 1974). Coefficients of these three subsets of explanatory variables are examined both together and separately.

H_4: $\gamma_{ij} = 0$ $i, j = 1, \ldots, 5$. Interactions between correlations linking endogenous variables are shown to be significant later in this chapter in the decomposition of correlations, so this hypothesis should be rejected.

H_5: $\delta_{sk} = 0$ for all s, k. This is the core of the meta-analysis. Acceptance of this hypothesis of no systematic effect of individual study characteristics implies regularities in the patterns of consumer choice processes that do not depend on setting.

Results. The ANOVA results are assessed with two tests (table 5–4) to illustrate an additional means for handling common or shared variance. The incremental ANOVA test is based on partial F ratios that contain no portion of the common variance in the numerator. This is a conservative test because it disregards shared variance completely except in the overall test of fit. The least conservative test is based on the contribution of each variable set considered separately, allowing each set to include its portion of common variance. This is analogous to tests on a series of simple correlations. The two approaches to testing in effect bracket the real explanatory effects of a factor. If factors are independent (for example, if the design is orthogonal), the tests are identical.

The ANOVA results are loaded in favor of rejecting the hypotheses of equality by the choice of dependent variables in the step-wise reduction. The less conservative tests further are loaded in favor of rejection by the inclusion of common variance.

Variables for which the null hypothesis is rejected by both tests include only the grand mean (such as $\mu \neq 0$) and the controllable exogenous variables (for example, $\beta_k \neq 0$, $k = 5, \ldots, 9$). Implications of numerical values of the particular significant ANOVA coefficients are discussed in the next section.

Acceptance of the null hypothesis of no effect for a set of ANOVA variables under both tests provides strong evidence that there is no systematic variability in the elasticities related to those variables. Variables for which the null hypothesis is accepted for both tests include study characteristics (such as $\delta_{sk} = 0$ for all s,k) and uncontrollable exogenous explanatory variables (chiefly sociodemographics; for example, $\beta_k = 0$, $k = 10, \ldots, 14$). General parametric patterns in these models are not sensitive to the many specific study characteristics (including country, type of product, wave of measurement, estimation procedure, or method of interviewing) that are often thought to have major effects on

Table 5–4
Summary of ANOVA Hypothesis Tests

Hypothesis	Hypothesized Parameter Values	Accept or Reject Null Hypothesis?		Implications of Conservative Test
		In Conservative Test Deleting Common Variance	In Least Conservative Test Incorporating Common Variance	
H_1	$\mu = 0$	Reject	Reject	Average elasticities are nonzero
H_2	$\alpha_i = 0; i = 1, \ldots, 4$	Accept	Reject	Elasticities do not vary over dependent variables[a]
H_3	$\beta_j = 0; j = 1, \ldots, 14$	Reject	Reject	Elasticities vary over explanatory variables
a.	$\beta_j = 0; j = 1, \ldots, 4$	Accept	Reject	Elasticities do not vary over causal endogenous variables[a]
b.	$\beta_j = 0; j = 5, \ldots, 9$	Reject	Reject	Elasticities for controllable exogenous variables are different from average
c.	$\beta_j = 0; j = 10, \ldots, 14$	Accept	Accept	Elasticities associated with sociodemographic factors do not differ from mean
H_4	$\gamma_{ij} = 0; i = 1, \ldots, 4$ $j = 1, \ldots, 4$	Accept	Reject	Elasticities do not vary systematically for specific pairings of endogenous system variables[a]
H_5	$\delta_{sk} = 0; k = 1, \ldots, 7$	Accept	Accept	Elasticities do not vary systematically over products, settings, interviewing methods or estimation procedures; pooling is plausible

Source: Reprinted by permission from "Patterns in Parameters of Buyer Behavior Models: Generalizing from Sparse Replication," John U. Farley, Donald R. Lehmann, and Michael J. Ryan, *Marketing Science*, 1, no. 2 (Spring 1982), Copyright 1982, The Institute of Management Sciences, 290 Westminster Street, Providence, RI 02903.

[a]Tests produce conflicting results.

how consumers make purchasing decisions. Together, the fact that these situational factors do not cause systematic variation in elasticities makes the pooling of elasticities over studies and settings plausible.

When the null hypothesis is accepted under the conservative test but rejected under the less conservative test, it is likely that shared variance plays a significant role. Variables for which this happened are the endogenous variables (explanatory and dependent) and interactions between them. The generally insignificant pattern of endogenous variable interactions is reinforced by the fact that only three of the original twelve candidate interaction variables survived the screening process. Model sensitivities to the endogenous variables (which constitute the core of the buyer behavior models) are approximately equal. Further evidence is needed to confirm this result, however, particularly for the interactions.

Individual ANOVA Coefficients. The strong effects of the controllable exogenous variables are reflected in the significant individual ANOVA coefficients (table 5–5), which show that two controllable variables (price and distribution) systematically contribute more to differences among elasticities than any other

Table 5–5
Significant Individual ANOVA Coefficients

	Number of Variables in Group	*Value of Coefficients*[*]
Coefficients of variables from significant ANOVA groupings		
Constant (grand mean)	1	0.228
Exogenous controllable variables	5	
Distribution		1.130
Price		−0.995
Coefficients of variables from nonsignificant ANOVA groupings		
Endogenous dependent variables	4	
Satisfaction		0.252
Endogenous explanatory variables	4	
Knowledge		0.351
Satisfaction		−0.488
Endogenous variable interactions	3	
Purchase with attitude		0.577
Exogenous noncontrollable variables	5	
None significant		
Study characteristics	6	
Two-stage least-squares estimation		0.230
$R^2_{adj} = 0.342$		

Source: Reprinted by permission from "Patterns in Parameters of Buyer Behavior Models: Generalizing from Sparse Replication," John U. Farley, Donald R. Lehmann, and Michael J. Ryan, *Marketing Science*, 1, no. 2 (Spring 1982), Copyright 1982, The Institute of Management Sciences, 290 Westminster Street, Providence, RI 02903.
[*]All significant at $\alpha = 0.05$.

individual variable. Advertising elasticities, by contrast, do not differ significantly from the grand mean.

The other individually significant ANOVA effects in table 5–5 are smaller but provide useful insights. In terms of variable pairings, the significant positive interaction of purchase and attitude reinforces general results from both large-scale consumer behavior and Fishbein-based models that link attitude and behavioral intention. The significant coefficient for two-stage least squares estimation indicates that TSLS produces larger elasticities on average than does ordinary least squares. This suggests that the numerical behavior of estimators rather than asymptotic statistical properties of alternative approaches to parameter estimation must be better understood in applications such as these (Farley 1967).

The fact that certain coefficients are not significant also has implications. Of special interest is β_{10}, the coefficient associated with past purchase (a measure of a lagged endogenous variable, behavior), consistently a significant predictor of endogenous system variables in these applications as well as in others (Farley and Ring 1972; Farley and Sexton 1982). The fact that this elasticity is not different from the grand mean indicates that these systems are not simply driven by past behavior. Significant again by their absence are any individual effects associated with product, country, interviewing method, or wave of measurement, implying that contextual factors have minimal systematic impact on estimated elasticities. Another way of looking at this result is that existing studies can reasonably provide first-cut estimates for a variety of products in a variety of settings and that the elasticities are relatively invariant with respect to measurement or estimation.

Implied System Behavior. Although it is possible to assess properties of each of the four individual systems under study here, the results of the meta-analysis add a level of generality to these properties. The behavior of the system depends on the values of system parameters. If the absolute values of the elasticities average unity, for example, a 1 percent shift on any structural variable will cause a 1 percent shift in those variables that it affects. Because of specified positive feedback loops, the endogenous variables will grow proportionally and continuously. Elasticities greater than 1 in absolute value will cause more rapid system divergence in response to external shock. By contrast, if the absolute values of system elasticities are less than unity, the system will respond less than proportionately to outside shock and will converge to a new equilibrium following a shift in one of the causal variables. If the elasticities are relatively small, the convergence will be rather rapid. If only some elasticities connecting endogenous variables are unity or greater in absolute value, the system may either diverge or converge, depending on the particular pattern of the relationships. More insight is provided by combining the results of the ANOVA and the values of the regression coefficients. Using the conservative tests, the elasticities associated with the endogenous variables are generally equal to the grand mean ($\mu = .29$, $\alpha_i = \beta_j = \gamma_{ij} = 0$ for all i and j and $k = 1, \ldots, 5$), indicating that the systems will generally converge fairly quickly when subjected to external shock. Values generally ranging from 0.2 to 0.4 were also found for significant elasticities relating endogenous variables in a model of households' adoption of family planning in eight countries (Farley and Sexton 1982).

The significant controllable exogenous variables have larger immediate impact on the systems. Distribution elasticities average 1.42 (1.13 plus the constant, 0.29), but an elasticity greater than 1 associated with an exogenous variable does not cause the systems to diverge. The negative price elasticity, averaging –0.707, does not change the conclusion of convergence and also contributes face validity to the general approach.

Within-Study Analysis of Summary Statistics: Direct Decomposition of a Correlation Matrix

An effective and relatively novel exploratory approach for initial stages of analysis involves decomposing the set of zero-order correlations of multiple measurements on multiple stimuli from a given study. This is a rather general approach in that the correlation matrix is also usually the starting point for estimation of explicit model parameters in literatures of the type being discussed here.

Different types of data configuration make different types of ANOVA models appropriate. Some possibilities are shown for illustration in a hypothetical correlation matrix involving two waves of panel measurements, with multiple indicators of a set of constructs (figure 5–2):

> For any single wave (or single wave study), a triangular correlation matrix such as I is present. For these correlations, it is possible to develop a model including both multiple measurements within construct and relationships between constructs. The approach is related to the analysis of correlations suggested by the multitrait, multimethod approach (Campbell and Fiske 1959).

> For a two-wave study using different respondents, two such triangles (I and II) are available. Insofar as measurement is on parallel constructs (for example, $K = M$) and each set of measurements is identical, a parallel ANOVA model can be estimated viewing the two triangles as replications. A similar approach can be used for two stimuli measured identically on either the same or different samples, which will also yield two triangular correlation matrices that can be viewed as replications.

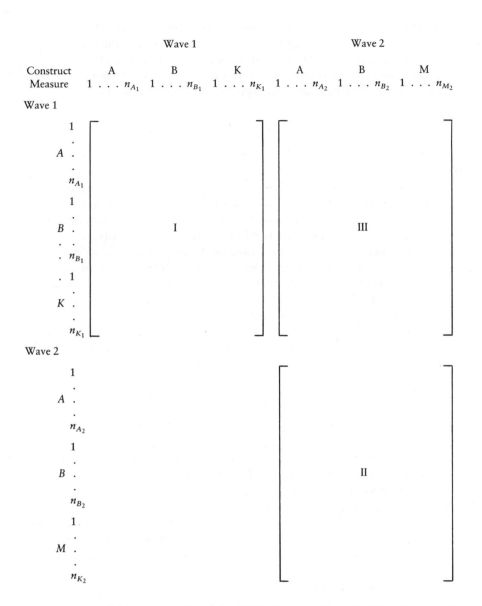

Source: Reprinted with permission from Donald R. Lehmann and John U. Farley, "Decomposing the Correlation Matrix in Panel Data," in Kent Monroe, ed., *Advances in Consumer Research*, 8 (1981), Washington: Association for Consumer Research.

Figure 5-2. Illustrative Two-Wave Multiconstruct, Multimeasure Correlation Matrix

Remeasurement on the same respondents either over stimuli in a cross-section or over time as in a panel (or both) produces rectangular correlation matrices like III, in addition to triangles I and II. When identical measurements are used on each wave or stimulus, III is square, and test-retest reliabilities of the measurements appear on the main diagonal.

Direct decomposition of the correlation matrix uses various features of constructs, repeated within-construct measurement, time, and stimuli to develop design patterns to be used in analysis of variance models for assessing patterns of systematic differences in arrays of correlations of the type shown in figure 5–2. The design of the ANOVA is idiosyncratic to a particular application, depending on the number of waves, the extent to which parallel measurements are used, and the extent to which correlations measured on different stimuli (usually brands) can reasonably be viewed as replications. Further, the number of available cross-wave and cross-stimuli matrices determines the number of replications available, which in turn determines the extent to which various second- and higher-order interactions can be incorporated into the ANOVA design.

For example, the correlations for two waves of measurements on the endogenous variables in the car model are shown in table 5–6. An ANOVA model including two-way interactions of a given correlation is:

$$r_{ijklm} = u + \alpha_i + \beta_j + \gamma_k + \delta_l + \phi_m + \xi_{nn} + \psi_{pq} + \epsilon_{ijklmnpqs} \qquad (5.2)$$

where $i = 1, 2$ brand of row and column variable; $j,k = 1, 2$ wave of row and column position in table 5–1, respectively; $l,m = 1, 2, 3, 4$ variables in row and column in table 5–1, respectively; $n = 1\text{–}1, 2\text{–}2, 3\text{–}3, 4\text{–}4$ indicating remeasurement on the same variable; $p,q = 1, 2, 3, 4$, $(p \neq q)$ interaction terms pairing different variables; and $s = 1, \ldots, 56$ the cells in the correlation matrix.

The model in equation 5.2 contains direct effects $(\alpha,\beta,\gamma,\delta,\phi)$ as well as interactions $(\xi \text{ and } \psi)$. Sometimes it is useful to fit the direct effects alone and then analyze the residuals for indications of significant interactions. Such a procedure indicated the presence of interactions in the present case (Lehmann and Farley 1981).

Regression procedures were used for estimation. The direct effect variables are binary and were coded $+1, -1$ so coefficients of a given effect sum to zero. Pair-wise interaction terms are formed by direct multiplication of the corresponding direct effects (brand, wave, and variable). The two brands are also viewed as replications of the same data-generating process. Two different specifications of ψ_{pq} are used: one symmetric (for example, $\psi_{pq} = \psi_{qp}$) and one in which the coefficients are not constrained to be equal.

Table 5–6
Simple Intervariable Correlations for Two Waves of Measurement on Volkswagen and Vega

Volkswagen

Construct	Wave 1				Wave 2			
	Intention	Attitude	Confidence	Knowledge	Intention	Attitude	Confidence	Knowledge
	Cross-Brand Correlations for Wave I[a]				*Within-Brand Cross-Time Correlations*			
Wave 1								
Intention		0.261	0.164	−0.097	0.266	0.184	0.138	0.015
Attitude	0.218		0.346	0.133	0.254	0.712	0.312	0.134
Confidence	0.211	0.444		0.302	0.133	0.291	0.488	0.215
Knowledge	0.050	0.338	0.270		−0.057	0.132	0.232	0.435
	Within-Brand Cross-Time Correlations				*Cross-Brand Correlations for Wave II[a]*			
Wave 2								
V E Intention	0.144	0.125	0.091	0.012		0.239	0.184	0.002
G Attitude	0.166	0.419	0.261	0.215	0.305		0.373	0.053
A Confidence	0.133	0.279	0.398	0.293	0.220	0.431		0.267
Knowledge	0.060	0.185	0.227	0.495	0.002	0.254	0.267	

Source: Reprinted with permission from Donald R. Lehmann and John U. Farley, "Decomposing the Correlation Matrix in Panel Data," in Kent Monroe, ed., *Advances in Consumer Research*, 8 (1981), Washington: Association for Consumer Research.
[a]Volkswagen above major diagonal and Vega below.

Table 5–7

Results of ANOVA Directly Decomposing Correlation Matrix Relating Measurements in Car Buyer Behavior Study

Source of Variation	Degrees of Freedom	Sum of Squares	F ratio
Brand (α_i)	1	0.00252	0.579
Wave in row and column (β_j, γ_k)	2	0.01555	1.787
Variable in row and column (δ_1, ϕ_m)	6	0.39256	15.040*
Reliabilities (ξ)	3	0.24010	18.398*
Interaction (ψ)			
Symmetric effect	3	0.26742	20.492*
Increment provided by asymmetry	3	0.00236	0.181
Error	37	0.16104	

Source: Reprinted with permission from Donald R. Lehmann and John U. Farley, "Decomposing the Correlation Matrix in Panel Data," in Kent Monroe, ed., *Advances in Consumer Research*, 8 (1981), Washington: Association for Consumer Research.
*Significant at $\alpha = 0.01$.

Results

Overall the ANOVA model in equation 5.2 explains 86.8 percent of the total variance among the correlations. The natural experimental design is not orthogonal, but the problem of shared variance is minimal because only 7.2 percent of the total explained variance was not explained by the direct effects and interactions in the ANOVA model. Specific results (table 5–7) included the following:

There was no significant change over time in the correlations, although the Vega was newly introduced. It appears that intervariable correlation structure becomes stable quite quickly, probably in part because the product class is well known and heavily advertised.

No significant differences were found between Vega and Volkswagen correlations despite the fact that the Vega was a new brand. In other words, interrelationships among these variables generalize over brands.

Significant differences were found in correlations involving different individual variables. This indicates that the variables are not simply one common factor but measure different constructs.

A significant test-retest effect was found, indicating reliability and/or the existence of a significant carryover effect for individual variables.

An interaction effect also existed for individual variable pairs, indicating the presence of some type of model linking the variables. A test for symmetry of interactions (for example, that the correlations of attitude and knowledge are the same for different wave pairings) shows that the interactions are symmetric. This implies that the interactions are stable over time.

Additional insights into the nature of the data are provided by the regression coefficients from the ANOVA. The analysis of the sums of squares indicates the existence of but not the direction of an effect. Consequently just reporting which coefficients are significant ignores the direction and magnitude of the effects that meta-analysis is designed to uncover. A significant effects model consisting only of those variables identified by the ANOVA just discussed is equivalent to pooling the sums of squares of the insignificant effects in table 5–7 with those of the residual error term. This model contains direct effects of variables, plus reliability and symmetric interaction terms. The coefficients (table 5–8) are in units of increment or decrement of correlation around the constant term, which estimates the ANOVA grand mean. Among the individual variables, correlations involving knowledge and attitude are incrementally larger, while correlations involving intention are incrementally negative and significant. The reliabilities add significant increments of correlation, while the interactions have modest negative effects.

It is important to note that mean values of the variables are not under study here; only basic relationships among variables as captured by the correlations are under study. This is a crucial point, since many critics of meta-analysis view it as comparing apples with oranges. What we assume, however, is not that the

Table 5–8
Regression Coefficients for Variables in Significant Effects Model

	Row		Column
Direct variable effects			
Intention	−0.088*		−0.120*
Knowledge	0.081*		0.077*
Attitude	0.029		0.068*
Reliability			
Intention		0.172*	
Knowledge		0.171*	
Attitude		0.083*	
Symmetric interactions			
Intention-Knowledge		0.000	
Intention-Attitude		−0.045*	
Knowledge-Attitude		−0.037	

R^2 = 0.848.
R^2_{adj} = 0.806.
Constant = 0.242.

Source: Reprinted with permission from Donald R. Lehmann and John U. Farley, "Decomposing the Correlation Matrix in Panel Data," in Kent Monroe, ed., *Advances in Consumer Research*, 8 (1981), Washington: Association for Consumer Research.
*Significant t statistic.

average rating of brand 1 on attitude is equal to the average rating of brand 2 on attitude (which they clearly were not) but that the relation of attitude to intention may be the same for both apples and oranges (brands 1 and 2), which do share certain similarities.

Within-Study Analysis of Raw Data: Varying Parameter Analysis

When raw data are available for meta-analysis and when the size of the natural experimental design is manageable, estimation of structural parameters (for example, equation 4.1) and meta-analytical parameters (equation 4.2) can be combined, resulting in simultaneous estimation of an augmented set of parameters including both the parameters of the original model and a set of meta-analytical variables. The augmented car buyer behavior model discussed in chapter 4 provides such an opportunity to incorporate the meta-analysis model in the estimation. Data requirements are simply that observations on the same variables be available over subsets of the data base so that identical measurements are available for all individuals and so that observations can be readily identified in terms of relevant groupings (for instance panel wave or group receiving a particular questionnaire).

Like the original analysis, estimation was done using equation-by-equation OLS, primarily because of its robustness, although multi-equation methods have been developed, and their behavior under various conditions is being studied (Carpenter and Farley 1984). Because one brand was evaluated by only half the sample, each brand was analyzed separately. The results test whether the coefficients differ by interviewing wave and sample group. The model was estimated separately for two brands because the samples responding about the two cars differed. If we restricted the sample to only those individuals who responded to both brands, we could then have included brand as an additional design variable in the meta-analysis. In this case, it makes better use of the data to compare results of one meta-analysis on each brand using different sample sizes. The results (table 5–9) indicate that the coefficients of the core model in equation 2.2 (the β's and γ's) are significant as expected, indicating that all the model parameters are not equal. On the other hand, neither means nor slopes associated with endogenous or exogenous variables differ over sampling waves or over groups who faced somewhat different questionnaires. From a meta-analytical point of view, this means that the results of the core model generalize and can be pooled across the waves and groups.

The pooling increases the power of tests for differences in slopes across brands in the context of the original model. Table 5–10 shows that the slopes of the endogenous variables are remarkably similar for the two brands. Only the carryover coefficients of intention and attitude are smaller for the new brand

Table 5–9
Patterns in Structural Parameters and Meta-Analysis Parameters Estimated Jointly for Car Buyer Behavior Model

	Null Hypothesis about Coefficients as Designated in Equation 3.2	Number of Significant Coefficients	Probability of This or a More Extreme Result[a]
Structural parameters			
Slopes of contemporaneous variables			
Endogenous variables	$\beta_{ij} = 0$	5 of 8	<1%
Exogenous variables	$\gamma_{ij} = 0$	15 of 44	<1
Slopes of lagged endogenous variables	$\gamma_{10} = 0$	8 of 8	<1
Meta-Analysis Parameters			
Differences in means of endogenous variables			
Over waves	$\alpha_{ij} = 0$	1 of 16	56
Over groups	$\delta_{ij} = 0$	2 of 16	19
Differences in slopes of endogenous variables			
Over waves	$\theta_{ij} = 0$	1 of 24	70
Over groups	$\xi_{ij} = 0$	1 of 16	56
Differences in slopes of exogenous variables			
Over waves	$\psi_{ijk} = 0$	4 of 76	53
Over groups	$\phi_{ijk} = 0$	7 of 76	4

Source: Reprinted with permission from John U. Farley, Donald R. Lehmann, Russell S. Winer, and Jerrold Katz, "Parameter Stationarity and 'Carry-Over Effects' in a Consumer Decision Process Model," *Journal of Consumer Research*, 8 (March, 1982):465–471.
[a]Binomial approximation assuming independence of estimates with $\alpha = 0.05$.

than for the established brand, and even these are of the same order of magnitude. This indicates a further degree of generalization: the parameters relating endogenous variables in the original model tend to be of the same size for different brands. These results thus reinforce those based on the simple correlations.

Discussion

Various approaches to meta-analysis have been demonstrated in this chapter. On those rare occasions when appropriately configured raw data are available, meta-analytic variables can be incorporated directly into a model. When the analysis must be based on a collection of summary statistics, a number of options are available, ranging from direct ANOVA decomposition of a full set of

Table 5–10
Coefficients of Contemporaneous and Lagged Endogenous Variables

	Dependent Variable							
	Intention		Attitude		Confidence		Comprehension	
	VW	Vega	VW	Vega	VW	Vega	VW	Vega
Coefficients of contemporaneous endogenous variables								
Attitude	.92[a] (.042)	.101[a] (.036)						
Confidence	.006 (.008)	.036 (.034)						
Comprehension			.194[a] (.077)	.102 (.096)	.496[a] (.132)	.438[a] (.116)		
Carryover effects								
Coefficient of lagged endogenous variable	.277[a]* (.027)	.210[a]* (.020)	.640[a]* (.022)	.565[a]* (.017)	.425[a] (.014)	.408[a] (.026)	.340[a] (.026)	.300[a] (.019)

Source: Reprinted with permission from John U. Farley, Donald R. Lehmann, Russell S. Winer, and Jerrold Katz, "Parameter Stationarity and 'Carry-Over Effects' in a Consumer Decision Process Model," *Journal of Consumer Research*, 8 (March, 1982):465–471.

Note: Standard errors in parentheses.

*Significant differences over brands.

[a]Significant at $\alpha = 0.05$.

correlations, through MANOVA when the dependent variable is multivariate and the literature well structured, to various ANOVA procedures when the data are not so well configured.

The significant coefficients of the general linear model (which constitutes the core of the analysis) indicate the extent to which a given factor in the natural experiment causes a parameter value to differ systematically from the mean of the overall population. An insignificant effect simply indicates that parameters measured under that condition do not vary significantly from the overall average. Some caution must be exercised in interpreting significance, however, because shared variance may mean that an ANOVA has considerable explanatory power not attributable to a specific factor, leading to a tendency to accept null hypotheses too frequently. Some approaches for dealing with shared variance are discussed in chapter 6.

Since the natural experimental design is for practical purposes never orthogonal and since the dependent variable set often has a large number of missing elements, regression programs ordinarily provide a more flexible approach to computation than do ANOVA programs, which are often structured along the lines of classical experimental designs and may not handle design imperfections well. Also, ANOVA programs frequently fail to provide the needed estimates of the coefficients in the linear model, and they often fail to provide overall measures of goodness of fit.

The analysis phase of meta-analysis depends heavily on the nature of the dependent variables, on the natural experimental design, and its proper configuration. Care and thought on these issues makes analysis easier and more likely to provide insights.

6
Using Information about Relationships among the Design Variables

In chapters 4 and 5, we showed that imperfections in the natural experimental designs produce two related substantive problems for meta-analysis: (1) inadequate sample sizes, relative to the number of potential elements, for dealing with all or even a large portion of interactions in a factorial design, and (2) explained variance which is shared by nonorthogonal factors in the natural design and cannot be attributed to specific factors and which indicates the presence of such interactions. The problems are related because much larger sample sizes are required to estimate a model containing interactions that represent the shared variance. Even if a relatively large set of studies is available, it must be configured in such a way that many cells of the design are represented; that is, a large number of studies with a particular combination of characteristics (for example, a large number of replications in one cell) may not increase the effective sample size.

Little can be done in most meta-analyses about inadequate sample sizes, provided that the collection of studies is reasonably exhaustive. The number of interactions in a factorial design will in practice usually swamp the number of studies available, and sample sizes (that is, the number of studies) generally cannot be increased enough by the meta-analyst through adding new models fit to existing data.

By contrast, shared variance (treated basically as a nuisance and often even eliminated or ignored by the classical statistical methods used in chapter 5) may contain some useful information that can be exploited. The purpose of this chapter is to examine some ways to capitalize on shared variance in a meta-analysis.

The approaches suggested here should not be confused with explicit specification in meta-analysis of interaction terms on the basis of theory, which should be the first step in dealing with shared variance. An example of this approach is the specification of interactions of endogenous dependent and explanatory variables in the buyer behavior meta-analysis in chapter 4.

Importance of Shared Variance

We have seen examples of meta-analysis in which shared variance is actually larger than variance that can be attributed to specific design variables (table 5–3), implying that the majority of information available in the natural experiment is effectively lost in conventional ANOVA.

Ideally, explanatory variables are independent of each other (figure 6–1), as they are, for example, in most classic experimental designs. In practice, however, the experimental designs implied by collections of marketing studies contain strong, generally substantive patterns of correlations among the design variables (for example, frequently purchased goods are usually studied with panel or audit data). In principle, a system of equations can be used to assess the impact of each variable, providing that the system is identified. However, it is usually hard to develop an unambiguous theoretical argument that one design variable causes another in patterns like those in figure 6–1. For example, it is hard to say that a decision to study a frequently purchased good causes the use of panel data. Conversely, the use of panel data necessitates studying frequently purchased goods and, given the tendency of researchers to seek available data before defining study objectives, this may be close to a causal relationship.

More often, it is reasonable to posit that two design variables are empirically confounded (figure 6–1), in some cases sequentially. Although treating confounding is not easy, there is a benefit in that the identification and specification problems associated with developing and estimating a causal model linking nominal independent variables are avoided.

This chapter describes four ways to use information about empirical confounding among the independent variables. Most existing approaches to dealing with shared variance focus on partitioning or assigning explanatory power in a significance testing framework to avoid understating the importance of a factor (Green, Carroll, and DeSarbo 1978). This chapter focuses instead on ways to make substantive use of patterns like those shown in figure 6–1.

Unlike the procedures described in chapters 4 and 5, these methods are still under development, and the results described in this chapter are close to feasibility tests. In fact, much of the material in this chapter has never been published because it was removed from journal articles at the request of reviewers and editors who generally lack our enthusiasm for shared variance as a useful information resource.

Showing Where Shared Variance Is Important and Where It Is Not

The first task in dealing with shared variance is to establish if and where it is important. Probably the best way to establish the overall importance of shared

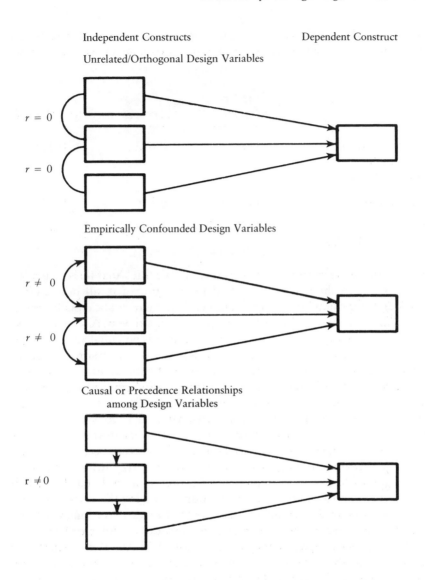

Figure 6–1. Alternative Patterns of Relationships in Design Variables

variance is with the approach used in chapter 5. The partial effects of each factor in the experiment are established by eliminating factors one at a time from the ANOVA and calculating the partial contribution of each factor to explanation of total variance. The difference between the total sum of squared error explained by all factors (the R^2 or coefficient of determination of an overall regression) and the sum of the partial explanations of each of the factors is the shared variance.

In the case of the meta-analysis of the econometric advertising results, for example, the relative importances calculated in this manner were as follows (table 5–3):

	Short-term Elasticity	Carryover	R^2 of Model
Explanatory power of factors in the experimental design	0.361	0.073	0.215
Shared variance	0.140	0.526	0.376
Total explanatory power (R^2) of ANOVA	0.501	0.599	0.591

Shared variance is clearly important in this case. (We think that this calculation of shared variance should be a standard result reported in all nondesigned ANOVA and regression.) However, shared variance may not be equally important for all or even most of the factors in a natural experiment. A relatively easy way to isolate those factors for which shared variance is potentially important is also to develop, as we did in chapter 5, a least conservative test for the set of experimental factors, a series of one-way analyses of variance for each factor.

The purpose of the least conservative tests is to see whether a factor plus any shared variance associated with it is significant. If the null hypothesis of no effect cannot be rejected even under this test, it is reasonable not to consider that factor further. Of course, the series of least conservative tests overstates the explanatory power of the experiment by double-counting the shared variance, so this elimination of totally unpromising factors is just the first step toward the other procedures described in this chapter. It is, however, a vital step because it eliminates the need to worry about interactions involving the variables eliminated as unpromising. This elimination saves vital degrees of freedom, which are used up quickly in examining a complex of interactions of higher orders.

Table 6–1, for example, contains a recast form of the ANOVAs on the buyer behavior meta-analysis shown in table 5–4. Further examination of shared variance should clearly involve the two experimental factors (the grand mean and exogenous factors) shown significant in the most conservative test. In fact, Monte Carlo analysis of complex factorial experiments has shown that the interactions tend to involve pairs of factors that are singly significant (Farley and Reddy 1984). The results indicate that research setting is not significant under the least conservative test, so this can be eliminated from consideration.

We also have contradictory results on the two tests (endogenous dependent variables and interaction of endogenous dependent and explanatory variables).

Without further analysis, we cannot be sure whether these factors with contradictory results are important or whether the contradictory results simply reflect explanatory power that each shares with a third factor that is important.

Combinatorial Partitioning of Shared Variance

Main effects ANOVA models like those used in chapter 5 assign shared variance of all sorts (from combinations involving just two design variables to those jointly involving all design variables) to a sort of statistical limbo where it is lost to the analysis unless an overall coefficient of determination is reported. One

Table 6–1
Summary of ANOVA Hypothesis Tests

Null Hypothesis	Accept or Reject Null Hypothesis?		
	ANOVAs of All Null Hypotheses Examined Together	One-Way ANOVAs on Each Hypothesis	Conflict?
Average elasticities are zero	Reject	Reject	No
Elasticities do not vary over dependent variables[a]	Accept	Reject	Yes
Elasticities do not vary over explanatory variables	Reject	Reject	No
Elasticities do not vary over causal endogenous variables[a]	Accept	Reject	Yes
Elasticities for controllable exogenous variables are not different from average	Reject	Reject	No
Elasticities associated with sociodemographic factors do not differ from mean	Accept	Accept	No
Elasticities do not vary systematically for specific pairings of endogenous system variables[a]	Accept	Reject	Yes
Elasticities do not vary systematically over products, settings, interviewing methods, or estimation procedures; pooling is plausible	Accept	Accept	No

Source: Reprinted by permission from "Patterns in Parameters of Buyer Behavior Models: Generalizing from Sparse Replication," John U. Farley, Donald R. Lehmann, and Michael J. Ryan, *Marketing Science*, 1, no. 2 (Spring 1982), Copyright 1982, The Institute of Management Sciences, 290 Westminster Street, Providence, RI 02903.

[a]Tests produce conflicting results.

solution is to try to assess certain interactions in the experimental design. It is sometimes possible to trace through selected interactions in order to isolate those in the experimental design that are key in producing shared variability. This will be productive only when comparison of the most conservative and least conservative tests produces different results, as they did with the buyer behavior results. This approach is feasible only when the number of degrees of freedom available is sufficient to estimate all of the interactions of all orders in the reduced set of variables being examined. Otherwise the partitioning cannot be carried out. This is why the process of elimination is so important. The Monte Carlo experiments indicate that most shared variance occurs in relatively low-order interactions, with two-way and a few three-way interactions dominant and with the significant interactions frequently associated with pairs of significant main effects (Farley and Reddy 1984). However, low-order interactions are so numerous in most meta-analyses, relative to the available sample size, that exhaustive assessment of even the low-order interactions is not feasible without the elimination step.

As an example, we return to the ANOVAs on the buyer behavior model summarized in table 6–1. The sums of squared error in elasticities from the buyer behavior models explained under the two tests by each of the five factors are as follows:

Design Variables	Least Conservative Test	Most Conservative Test
Endogenous dependent variables	3.02*	1.34
Endogenous explanatory variables	3.60*	2.06
Endogenous interactions	2.70*	0.66
Controllable and uncontrollable exogenous variables	7.30*	6.44*
Study characteristics	2.74	2.56
Total associated with single factors		13.06*
Shared variance		3.02
Total sum of squares explained		16.08*

*Significant at $\alpha = .05$.

It is clear that the design variables most affected by shared variance involve endogenous variables. It is also clear that the two tests produce such similar results for the exogenous variables and for the study characteristics that no further probing of them is needed—that is, they are minimally involved in the shared variance in the system. Being able to eliminate part of the design variables is important because the number of combinations must generally be reduced before enumeration is practical.

Explained variance from the remaining three categories of variables can be further decomposed, using successive steps of elimination of two- and three-way combinations of design variables such as that used in developing the most conservative test but this time using only dependent and explanatory endogenous variables plus their interactions as design variables. This process of decomposition is somewhat tedious, and it also can get quite complex. For example, there are thirty-one combinations of one, two, three, four, and five effects in the relatively small set of five variable designs. (The thirty-second combination in this 2^5 problem involves the sum of squared error under omission of all design variables—for example, the ordinary variance.) Further, there are not nearly enough degrees of freedom available to probe deeply into each of the individual effects. In this case of just three remaining design variables, however, analysis can be done by enumeration of the seven combinations: the three direct effects, three pair-wise interactions, and one three-way interaction.

The result of such a decomposition is shown in figure 6–2, which contains error explained by each variable alone, by the three variable pairings, and by all three variables in concert. (It is generally not useful to try to create a Venn diagram with more than three variables.) Although some variance is explained by all these combinations, it is clear that relationships involving first-order interactions are key contributors to shared variance, and the cause should be probed in more depth. Perhaps the use of the endogenous explanatory variables in the denominator of the estimated elasticities causes a sort of nonlinearity to creep into the meta-analysis. It is also interesting that the highest-order intersection is small. If a series of meta-analyses indicate that higher-order interactions are unimportant, combinatorial partitioning will become more practical because it can concentrate, say, on just pairs and combinations of three design variables.

Although tedious, it seems likely that this sort of combinatorial probing procedure will produce more interesting results than will the various decision rules developed for distributing shared variance with the goal of obtaining more realistic test results (Green, Carroll, and DeSarbo 1978).

A Gestalt Approach to Meta-Analysis: Identifying Patterns of Similar Observations Based on the Design Variables

The meta-analyses in chapter 5 concentrated on direct effects of individual design variables, leaving explained variance shared by combinations of explanatory variables to be handled somehow, such as with the sort of decomposition

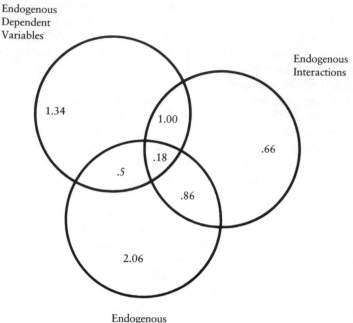

Figure 6–2. Sum of Squared Error in the Elasticities in Buyer Behavior Models Explained by Various Combinations of Factors

just discussed. A recently developed alternative approach (Capon, Farley, and Lehmann 1985) involves starting with the idea that there will be natural groupings (or gestalts) of observations that can be identified and profiled. Inferences can then be made by using characteristics of the group in which an observation belongs in place of the design variables in the meta-analysis proper. When one group is shown to be significantly different from the others, its profile can be examined in detail. The steps in the procedure are as follows:

Step 1. Observations are placed into more or less homogeneous groups using conventional cluster analysis of design variables.

Step 2. Since there is generally uncertainty about which group a particular observation belongs to, estimated probabilities that each observation belongs to each group are computed using discriminant analysis with as many groups as there were clusters identified in step 1. Because of the way the clusters are formed, the discriminant functions will generally reclassify the observations into clusters almost without error.

Step 3 (optional). If the design variables themselves can be divided naturally into more than one group based on substantive considerations, clusters of observations can be identified separately for each subgroup of design variables (step 1), and probabilities of cluster membership can be similarly computed for each group of design variables (step 2). A table can then be developed showing joint cluster membership to see how the clusters built on the two subsets of design variables relate to one another.

Step 4. For the meta-analysis itself, regressions are run using the same dependent variables defined as in chapter 2, but the set of probabilities of cluster membership developed in step 2 replaces the design variables as the independent variables. Profiles for clusters that turn out to have significant impact on the dependent variable (for example, on the meta-analysis) are then examined.

An alternative and somewhat simpler approach is to use dummy variables indicating cluster membership(s) (step 1 or step 3) directly in the regressions (step 4). In this case, step 2 is eliminated. The problem with this is that an observation with about equal probability of belonging to two or more clusters is assigned to the cluster that happens to be associated with the highest probability. Using the estimated probabilities from step 2 would partially assign that observation to more than one cluster. In practice, the clustering in step 1 usually produces one membership probability of 0.75 or greater for each observation, so the result of this simpler approach is often about the same as the probabilistic approach incorporating step 2.

As an example, chapter 5 indicated that the design variables and research environments were related in the study of econometric advertising results. Since the design variables are categorical, estimation of the links by simultaneous regression is complicated. Before trying to estimate causal or precedence links among the individual variables, it may be useful to generate profiles of observation (through cluster analysis) and then see how these are related to the dependent variables. A set of key design elements divides naturally into the two groups (table 6–2): thirteen variables related to the choice of what to study called environmental variables (definitions, situation, product, location, level, time period, media, and so on) and twelve variables related to the technical characteristics of the study, called design variables (definitions, specifications, estimation method, and others). In a world characterized by strong, competing research traditions but with the general absence of testing of competing models, the environmental design variables might form a small number of tight and distinct groupings, the technical design variables might similarly cluster, and each environmental cluster might map mainly onto one of the technical design clusters.

Table 6–2
Two Groupings of Design Variables in the Econometric Advertising Studies

Environmental Variables	Design Variables
Products	Definitions
Frequently purchased product	Dependent variable is market share
Food product	Dependent variable is sales
Durable product	Advertising measured as share
Other nondurables	Advertising measured as per capita
Mature product	
Data	Model Specification
Brand level	Carryover effect included
Monthly or weekly data	Other marketing variables included
Bimonthly or quarterly data	Price included
Pooled data	Exogenous variables included
Aggregate advertising	Multiplicative structure
Television advertising separate	
Location	Estimation
United States	OLS
Europe	Multistep single equation
	Nonlinear single equation

Alternatively, such clustering of environmental and technical variables might also occur because of some combining in nature—for example, studies of frequently purchased products (usually studied with time series of audit or panel data) generally incorporate carryover effects in multiplicative models. The result in either case would be highly confounded environmental and design variables.

Forming Groups of Similar Observations

Separate cluster analyses on the environmental and design variable groups, developed using the Howard-Harris algorithm on each group, produced seven apparently significant clusters for the environmental groups and six significant clusters for the design variables. Each of these clusters has its own profile in terms of the within-group means of each explanatory variable, but these profiles are interesting only for those clusters that differ from others in the meta-analysis.

Probabilities of Cluster Membership

Probabilities of cluster membership computed as part of standard k-class discriminant analysis are used as the independent variables in regressions that constitute the meta-analysis itself. The discriminant analyses simply assess the ability of the independent variables on which the clusters are based to classify each observation in a cluster. Given the way that the clusters are formed, the reassignment of observations into clusters by the discriminant functions is generally almost perfect. In this case, for example, only 6 assignments of 128 were different for the design variables, and only 8 of 128 were different for the environmental variables.

Analysis of Joint Cluster Membership

Choice of variables for cluster identification is generally based on substantive considerations—for example, variables controlled by researchers as against the uncontrollable variables like those discussed in chapter 2. When more than one clustering is done (as it is here), however, the groupings may be related. Table 6–3 shows considerable but not perfect correspondence of observations in corresponding clusters. At the one extreme, 10 observations group with one another perfectly in clusters 5A and 3B. In three other cases, all or nearly all of the observations in clusters 4A, 6A, and 7A, respectively, also appear in 4B, 2B, and 5B clusters, although the reverse is not the case. The fact that joint membership never exceeds four groups in any case also indicates considerable grouping. In fact, choosing the largest member in each row as an indicator, 77 of the 128 observations can be arranged in six common cells based on one row and one column group.

Meta-Analysis Using Probability of Cluster Membership

The regression coefficients for the probabilities of belonging to each of the thirteen clusters are shown in table 6–4. It appears that the clustering did little to provide additional insights about the short-term advertising response, for which shared variance (table 5–6) was a minimal problem. For both of the other dependent variables in the meta-analysis (for which shared variance in the ANOVA was dominant), the clustering does provide some possibly useful

Table 6–3
Patterns of Joint Membership in Design and Environmental Clusters

		B. Environmental Clusters						
		1	*2*	*3*	*4*	*5*	*6*	*N*
	1	13			9			22
	2	1	13		4		10	28
A.	3		3		6	11	3	23
Design	4	1			19			20
clusters	5			10				10
	6		7					7
	7					18		18
	N	15	23	10	38	29	13	128

Table 6–4
Regression Coefficients for Probabilities of Cluster Memberships

Design Variable Clusters

Dependent Variables in Meta-Analysis

		Short-Term Advertising Elasticity	Carryover Coefficient	R^2
Probability of belonging to cluster	1	−0.13	−0.34	0.36*
	2	0.12	−0.12	0.33*
	3	−0.03	0.29*	0.05
	4	0.10	0.32*	−0.23*
	5	−0.21*	0.14	−0.17
	6	−0.04	−0.28*	−0.13
	7	0.19	0.00	−0.22*

	Short-Term Advertising Elasticity	Carryover Coefficient	R^2
Intercept	0.16*	0.01*	0.43*
Coefficient of determination	0.25*	0.35*	0.26*

Environmental Variable Clusters

Dependent Variables in Meta-Analysis

		Short-Term Advertising Elasticity	Carryover Coefficient	R^2
Probability of belonging to cluster	1	−0.07	0.68*	−0.02
	2	−0.01	−0.35	−0.09
	3	−0.12	0.20	−0.33*
	4	0.18	−0.08	0.06
	5	0.12	−0.36*	0.08
	6	−0.12	−0.09	0.25*

*Significant at α = .05.

insight. Based on joint characteristics, table 6–5 indicates, for example, that goodness of fit particularly varies with a rather complex combination of characteristics. Fit tends to be higher in multiplicative models when OLS is used and when several other explanatory variables are included—all commonsense results but much richer conclusions than those reached in chapter 5. Similarly, carryover is higher under OLS in multiplicative models and for frequently bought products when measurement is also frequent (for example, when aggregation problems are minimal). This gestalt approach, of course, leads to loss of identity of particular design variables, but this loss also occurs when explained variance is highly shared by a set of design variables.

The gestalt approach thus appears to be most useful when the conventional ANOVAs indicate a high degree of shared variance.

An ANOVA Approach to Causal Confounding and Precedence

The gestalt results just discussed can be extended further if the relationships between the variable sets are viewed as ordered. If a researcher selecting a particular level in one variable is disproportionately likely to select a particular level in another variable, causal relationships or at least precedence relationships may exist among the independent variables in the natural experiment. A researcher choosing to study advertising effectiveness for a frequently purchased good may use certain design features that are chosen simultaneously, such as bimonthly (audit) or quarterly (panel) data. This choice of data may then govern model specification of controllable variables because of availability (for example, prices or exogenous variables) and structure (for example, carryover effects). This section suggests a regression approach for dealing with precedence among the independent variables in the experimental design. This causal or precedence structure of research environment affecting technical design can be embedded in the ANOVAs by a two-step process:

1. Regressions are used to predict the design variables later in the causal chain using the variables with precedence (in this case the environmental variables) as explanatory variables. These regressions do not use the dependent variable of the meta-analysis.

2. ANOVA is then used to isolate the indirect effects of the precedent (environmental) variables on advertising elasticity by replacing the values of the subsequent (design) variables with estimated values from the regressions. The impact of the subsequent (design) variables is thus divided into two categories: that attributable to their relationships with environmental variables through estimated values from the regressions and that attributable to

Table 6–5
Significant Differences in Cluster Probability Measures

	Design Variable Clusters			Environmental Variable Clusters	
Cluster	Significant	Main Cluster Characteristics	Cluster	Significant	Main Cluster Characteristics
1	R^2 is higher	Market share dependent Price and other marketing variables specified Newer products OLS or nonlinear estimates Multiplicative model television advertising	1	Carryover is higher	Frequently purchased Nondurables Weekly or monthly data Brand level
2	R^2 is higher	Sales is dependent Advertising defined per capita Price, exogenous variables, and other marketing variables specified Media aggregated	3	R^2 is lower	Not United States or Europe Product level Monthly or weekly data
3	Carryover is higher	OLS or nonlinear single equation Multiplicative model	3	Carryover is lower	Aggregate advertising United States Food
4	Carryover is higher and R^2 is lower	Sales is dependent Advertising defined per capita Multiplicative model	7	R^2 is higher	Frequently purchased Food Infrequently measured
5	Short-term Response is lower	Sales is dependent Advertising defined per capita Media are aggregated			
7	R^2 is lower	Market share is dependent Advertising is defined as share Multiplicative model Exogenous variables specified Nonlinear estimation Pooled data Media aggregated			

incremental contributions of the technical variables represented by the residuals from that regression.

The procedure is illustrated here using short-term elasticity as the dependent variable and a set of design variables that were shown significant in chapter 5 as independent variables. The six research environment variables used in the study were food product, U.S. data, European data, bimonthly data, monthly data, and pooled data. The three model specification variables used were if exogenous variables were included, if an advertising carryover coefficient was included, and if a multiplicative model was used.

Table 6–6 contains beta coefficients with the three model specification variables treated as dependent. Because the dependent variables in this step are discrete, predictive power (R^2) is depressed, and the coefficients should be interpreted only as directional. However, the regression coefficients indicate a pattern of strong association between the two variable sets consistent with the gestalt results discussed previously.

The reformulated ANOVA (figure 6–3) for the nine variables produces an R^2 of 0.4, close to the 0.5 for the entire variable set (table 5–3). The partitioning of the explanatory power of the technical design variables assigns the majority of their importance (including variance shared over the two variable sets) to systematic elements related to the research environments (for example, the regression estimates), although the residuals add a significant increment of explanatory power. The impact of the precedent design variables thus appears to be even larger than previously indicated because of decisions that follow from their choice and which subsequently affect the results.

Like the combinatorial and gestalt approaches, this procedure has the

Table 6–6
Beta Coefficients of Research Environment Variables Significant in the ANOVAs in Regressions Explaining Model Specification

	Model Specification Variable (Dependent)		
Research Environment Variables (Explanatory)	Exogenous Variables Included	Advertising Carryover Included	Multiplicative Models Used
Food product	0.13	0.16	0.02
United States	0.28**	0.31**	0.08
Europe	−0.07	−0.31**	0.67**
Bimonthly data used	−0.35**	0.04	0.58**
Monthly data used	0.34**	−0.22**	−0.17**
Pooled data used	0.02	0.08	−0.24**
Adjusted R^2	0.34**	0.14*	0.47**

*Significant at $\alpha = .01$.
**Significant at $\alpha = .05$.

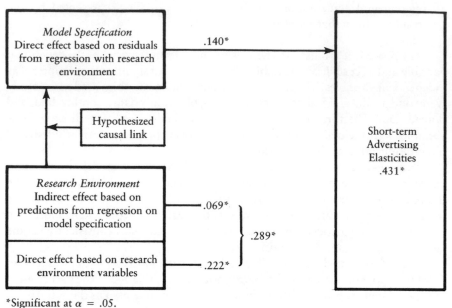

*Significant at $\alpha = .05$.
Variables listed in Table 6–2.

Figure 6–3. Fraction of Overall Variability in Short-Term Advertising Elasticities Explained by Various Elements in the "Causal" ANOVA

advantage of using information on shared variance caused by defects in the natural experiment but lost in the classical ANOVA analysis. It has the further advantage of injecting a sense of causation into the experimental design. Further, it is relatively easy to expand the approach to using more than two groupings in the design variables through the use of simultaneous modeling procedures.

Results of this procedure are best viewed as indicative, however, since assignment of the design variables in causal or precedence order determined to a large degree the assignment of the shared variance to the causal or preceding factor. Further, the regressions used nominal dependent variables, violating some assumptions of regression.

Summary

This chapter has discussed four methods for probing more deeply and substantively into shared variance in the natural experimental design of a meta-analysis:

isolating combinations of factors with shared variance, combinatorial partitioning of parts of the design, a gestalt approach for using membership in homogeneous subgroups of the sample in the meta-analysis, and an approach to modeling causal confounding and precedence. The methods discussed here are still in their developmental stage; much more work is needed to perfect them, but we think that meta-analysis can be made richer by further development of these methods. The four methods are illustrative and by no means exhaust the possibilities for creative use of information available to a meta-analyst.

7
A Meta-Analytic Overview

Meta-analysis is not a technique or a research tool, nor is it a specialized approach to a subclass of structured research problems. Meta-analysis is, rather, a way of thinking that is useful and efficient in terms of the use of available information.

Meta-analysis is broadly applicable in terms of guiding research design and interpreting results. It is also a logical extension of the multitrait, multimethod approach (Campbell and Fiske 1959) so widely accepted in social psychology.

Meta-analysis is, however, a way of thinking that is likely to be alien to the researcher in marketing, regardless of background. First, meta-analysis almost always involves null hypotheses other than absence of effect or zero values for parameters. Meta-analysis presumes the existence of a systematic signal. As a result, some nonconventional statistical thinking is needed although conventional statistical procedures are generally used.

Second, meta-analysis is cast empirically in the form of a natural experiment, which may be an alien way of thinking for those with training in formal experimental design. Defects in this natural design relative to a classic design are often important and difficult to deal with.

Third, meta-analysis starts with the basic notion that any given piece of research fits into an overall framework, a view that no doubt will run counter to the rugged individualism of most researchers.

Fourth, meta-analysis takes the view that any piece of work, however distantly related to a field of inquiry, may contain some information that will help provide prior values for future work. For example, sensitivities of sales to price, advertising, and distribution (linked together through the Dorfmann-Steiner 1954 theorem and through other general equilibrium relationships as well) may contribute materially to the understanding of each other. At a minimum, this robs the author of a lead sentence starting "Little is known about . . .".

Fifth, meta-analysis requires that the researcher think explicitly about the overall role of a given study in developing knowledge and hence about the major issues in the field. A study will contribute more to basic knowledge about a field if it fills an empty cell in the natural experimental design than it will if it essentially repeats previous work in a cell already occupied. (Exact replication is, of course, desirable to establish reliability, but exact replication is rare.)

Finally, meta-analysis often requires a new mental set. In our experience, the first reaction of a researcher to a meta-analysis is one of real interest, but that interest is generally accompanied by the remark that it cannot be done in his or her field. The objections generally focus on points that are in fact helpful for the meta-analysis, illustrating the new mental set required: noncomparability of studies, which in fact ensures that environmental variables exist for structuring the natural experiment; dissimilar measurement, which again means methodological design variables exist, although means to make the outputs of the various studies comparable will be required; and a small number of studies. Sample sizes in meta-analysis are often small relative to the number of potential design variables. It is important to remember, though, that even one existing study can be helpful in establishing priors and making judgments about research design. In general, meta-analysis is more broadly applicable than it appears at first.

Steps in a Meta-Analysis: Summary

The basic steps that are involved in a meta-analysis are laid out in figure 1–2 and followed through in examples in chapters 2 through 6. Each application is somewhat different; each can contribute to the base of knowledge about both the substantive matters dealt with by the population of studies and about what to look for in a meta-analysis. The steps in a meta-analysis are as follows:

1. Collecting results to form the dependent variable(s) of the meta-analysis. These may be averages (such as mean purchase rates or incomes), percentages (such as response rate to mail surveys or fraction of purchase of favorite brand), or model parameters (advertising or price elasticities). It is important to search for results outside the basic publications in a field, including those that have not been published—perhaps from industry or (especially) papers that have been rejected because the results do not seem to fit in (Rosenthal 1979).

2. Identifying elements of the natural experimental design to form the independent variables of the meta-analysis. These will ordinarily involve a combination of methodological features of the studies and characteristics of the research environment. The design variables are generally derived by combining received theory with suggestions often made by authors of the

individual studies describing the need to expand to new methodologies and new environments. In particular, careful attention should be paid to likely interactions in the design since the degrees of freedom required for assessment of interactions of all orders that are implied by the design far exceed the available sample size.

3. Analyzing the experimental design. This step involves an empirical assessment of the natural experiment in terms of the size of the implied factorial design associated with it (a theoretical calculation) and of the empirical dimensionality of the design itself (a numerical assessment associated with the invertibility of the cross-product of the design matrix).

4. Performing the meta-analysis. Only when key characteristics of the design are understood should the meta-analysis itself proceed. In general, the natural experiment will be shown to be nonorthogonal, so analysis will require some form of nonorthogonal analysis of variance or covariance procedure. If studies offer a well-structured set of multiple dependent outcomes, MANOVA or MANCOVA will probably provide the most insights. Sometimes pooling of results from a variety of experimental conditions may be required to make meta-analysis feasible. On rare occasions where the raw data are appropriately structured and available, meta-analysis can be built directly into the process of fitting model parameters by modeling the parameters to vary with the design variables of the meta-analysis.

5. Expanding the analysis to attempt to bring in more richness in terms of such factors as precedence relationships, causal ordering, or high probability of joint occurrence among the independent variables. Relative to the more conventional analytical approaches, this area is in a state of early development. It will gain enormously from more applications and refinements.

Implications of Meta-Analytic Thinking for Design of Individual Studies

The meta-analytic thought process has two major implications for individual studies. First, individual studies should be designed to be different in some important way (research environment, model specification) from past research. Perfect replications make it impossible to disentangle the potential causes (such as model or measurement method) of a result. Since most replications end up differing in some way (in product category, time period, or some other factor) anyway, it is better to plan for interesting variations than to be saddled with an unintended and uninteresting one.

This means that, for example, studies that assess the carryover effect of advertising using noneconometric methods (such as laboratory experiments or even case analyses) are likely to be useful in establishing generalizations if they in fact exist and if a comparable measure of the dependent variable is available. It suggests programmatic research is appropriate and that the program should be set by the needs of the individual field of research rather than simply by the proclivities of the researcher.

Second, individual studies should be designed as mini-meta-analyses. This is an extension of the competitive model testing school of thought, which suggests that different measurement methods, subjects, products, etc., should be included in a study and differences in results tested analytically. This thought runs counter to the tradition of experimentalists to keep all but a few factors constant and the feeling of people in the industry that there is something unique about their business ("Mouthwash is totally different from toothpaste"). The researcher, however, is in a win-win situation, since either the idea generalizes (to high- and low-involvement products), which is interesting, or there are differences (daytime ads work differently from nighttime television ads), which is also interesting. For the field, it makes possible conclusions on the extent to which generalizations are appropriate, as well as carefully controlled within-study comparison of methods, models, and other factors. Overall, the meta-analytic thought process argues for complexity and its attendant messiness (but not sloppiness or carelessness) as opposed to simplicity and clean, neat studies. Put differently, in addition to learning precisely about something simple of minor importance, it is also useful to learn approximately about complex issues.

Meta-Analysis and Laws in Marketing Response

We are taught that markets and products are so different that each must be analyzed separately. At some level, this is true. But meta-analysis seems to be teaching that a great deal generalizes. Patterns of consistency in marketing response are emerging in even the handful of meta-analyses of response models available in marketing. These are beginning to take on a sort of pattern resembling laws, at least in the context of primitive measurement devices.

The meta-analyses, which are generally based on a relative handful of design variables, explain over half of the interstudy variability in model response measures—about the level we tend to anticipate in aggregate cross-sectional models (Farley and Howard 1975).

The biggest systematic differences in response measures seem to be associated with model specification, including both functional form and the inclusion or exclusion of explanatory variables. The latter is apparently due in large part to the fact that variables in marketing are generally correlated, so systematic inclusion or omission of certain variables will alter results for standard statistical reasons.

Technical issues such as estimation and measurement, although important in principle, seem to have a relatively minor impact on estimated response measures.

Settings (product, sample, and so forth) seem to produce even smaller differences in results. In other words, response seems more nearly comparable from market to market than we generally expect it to be. When there are differences, they are generally in the expected direction. It is important to stress that we are not saying that income levels in Kenya, Argentina, and the United States are the same or that per capita sales levels of the products are the same; the meta-analysis simply says that income elasticities do not vary widely over the countries at the current state of market development and that something can be learned about one country from estimates derived in another. For example, similar response patterns have been reported in family planning models for eight countries with very different levels of socioeconomic measurements (Farley and Sexton 1982).

We are also beginning to build up some quantitative generalizations, which can be used as a benchmark against which to judge new results.

Parameters in the Fishbein models, all from studies using obtrusive measurement methods, average 0.45 for ω_1 and 0.3 for ω_2, with little systematic variation that could be explained by the meta-analysis. A recently completed study using unobtrusive measurement produced a value of 0.3 for ω_1 and 0.2 for ω_2, perhaps the beginning of a new stream of research on the impact of measurement method on model parameters. This in turn could help link experimental results to results that might be expected in a natural setting.

The short-term advertising elasticities in the published econometric models average about 0.2 and are a bit higher in Europe. By contrast, a particular European advertiser has fit a set of similar models with much lower elasticities—perhaps a diagnostic about quantity or quality of advertising.

The elasticity of purchase (or intention) with regard to attitude averages about 0.3 in the published buyer behavior models. A recently completed study of senior manufacturing executives found an attitude-intention elasticity of well over 1.0 associated with a highly technical product. The system is thus highly responsive but also potentially highly volatile in case of a downward shift in attitude. The potential upside gain in this case is severely limited because attitude is already highly favorable toward the producer durable under study. Similarly, a controlled field experiment in Singapore produced estimated attitude-intention elasticities near unity for a set of consumer products, which may indicate even more leverage of attitude on behavior than was previously thought.

Carryover coefficients (coefficients of lagged dependent variables in time series advertising models) seem with great consistency to take on values in the range of 0.3 to 0.5—a curiosity since the values seem independent of measurement period. They also seem fairly independent of what is being carried over:

consumption, purchase, intention, knowledge, sales, attitude, and so forth. A recent study of soft drinks found an average carryover of 0.39 in household-level consumption models, but carryover turned out to average 0.05 for about half of the sample households and about 0.6 for the other half. Aggregate carryover models may thus mask important heterogeneities over observations or over time.

This leads us to a key point that bears repeating: the null hypotheses of zero for model parameters in future studies of these types make neither substantive nor statistical sense. Once the notion that the null hypothesis of parameters equal to zero is abandoned, meta-analysis provides not only a more meaningful null hypothesis but also a prior for Bayesian analysis. By taking the forecast parameter values from the meta-analysis as the prior and a given study as the data, each study can lead to a posterior prediction-hypothesis for future research. Similarly when search procedures are used in estimating parameters (such as when maximum likelihood procedures are used to find the parameters of diffusion models), meta-analysis provides good starting values for the search and can improve the efficiency of the estimation procedure. Thus the results of meta-analysis not only summarize past work but also provide a means for more efficient parameter estimation in future studies.

Managerial Implications

Certain areas in market research implicitly depend heavily on meta-analytical thinking. For example, return rates for mail questionnaires are routinely estimated based on past studies that are seldom strictly comparable. This sort of rudimentary meta-analysis seems natural to those involved, although it is usually accompanied by some general discussion of comparability.

Meta-analysis of the type we are discussing is much more difficult for the manager or researcher to internalize. But these more advanced forms of meta-analysis hold more immediate promise for market researchers than for marketing managers. Nonetheless, some substantive patterns are emerging from our work already that may turn out to be immediately useful.

Implications for Marketing Managers' Use of Existing Research

Marketing managers tend to think that markets are different in salient ways until they are proved the same. Besides the important logical violation of conventional scientific method implied by this view, it is also antithetical to the outlook of the meta-analyst who looks for general laws based on the observation of past studies. Newton observed $f = ma$, a generalization of many specific situations. The practicing manager stands to learn a significant amount from a slightly broader view; the payoff could be enormous. Complex field experiments and test markets are undependable, costly, and time-consuming, and meta-analysis of existing market research can be at least a partial substitute. Many products are targeted at the same buyers and pass through the same channels with the same type and amount of promotional pressure. Surely there are other similarities that might be exploited.

We are finding patterns of extraordinary similarity in terms of market response to advertising for products in similar classes and at similar points in the product life cycle. Durables seem to follow similar patterns in different countries, which suggests that forecasts based on analogies (an application of meta-analysis) make sense in the international marketplace. Relatively mature products in slow-growth markets, regardless of location, seem to be similarly sluggish in terms of response to marketing effort. Thus if some data are available for products that are somehow similar, they may help managers make order-of-magnitude estimates of market responsiveness for their product.

Decision calculus models such as ADBUDG are basically user-friendly meta-analysis forecasting techniques. These models specify the key variables, the mathematical form of the relation between the variables, and (at least in the default options) the parameters of the models. A manager can customize these models by varying some of the parameters (for example, by assuming one's advertising is 10 percent more effective than one's competitors') but basically plays what-if games with the levels of the key variables.

In our search for applications of certain kinds of models in industry, we found that research may be available but not cataloged well. Managers should not give up if the first answer about availability of studies is negative. Although theirs may be the only division in the company that makes a particular product, theirs is probably not the only one with experience with certain types of markets.

Managers should let researchers know that within reasonable limits they will listen about results of research on product classes with certain similarities to those that the former are managing. This rather loose framing of requests may allow researchers to be more creative. The costs are very low and the potential gains high.

If managers are in a great hurry and cannot execute a new piece of research, they should think about using some sort of averaging of what is available. Many of the so-called simulated test market models available commercially simply use such averages of price, promotion, or advertising sensitivities to create benchmarks. (We do not recommend this procedure in general, but it is superior to guessing or to killing a promising project because of the uncertainty.)

Managers should try to get used to asking what is similar about markets rather than what is different. This will require a great deal of discipline, but it is basically how consultants go about assessing new or unfamiliar markets. Consultants almost always try to find familiar analogous situations. Managers can save time, frustration, and money and sometimes get better work by seeking out the analogies themselves.

Implications for Market Researchers Who Want
Marketing Managers to Use Their Work

Thinking along the lines of meta-analysis can produce specific benefits for practicing researchers.

In designing research, it is useful to think in terms of general constructs that are likely to recur and are in general comparable.

Although it may be appealing to think one's situation is unique (and hence one's expertise is invaluable), in general it is not. As the proverb goes, those who ignore history are doomed to repeat its mistakes.

There are enormous potential benefits from calibrating the relation of research results to actual results. This calibration can be enhanced by making all studies comparable by using a single type of attitude or intention question, eliminating variance due to measurement variability about which managers are particularly suspicious. Calibration over a set of studies will also make the researcher more confident in point estimates, which is what the manager is generally interested in.

Researchers should try to report some results from every study in terms of scaleless measures that are comparable over studies. Correlations are scaleless, and we find that marketing managers can often understand correlation coefficients—provided that they don't face too many at the same time. We also suggest that looking at levels of attitude and intention without looking at the correlation between them wastes information.

Managers tend to think hierarchically. Packaged goods managers, for example, tend to think awareness → knowledge → trial → repurchase. Such a paradigm can easily and naturally be built into reporting results of many studies, using some simple correlational measures.

Researchers should consider having evaluations of products made on sufficiently general attributes that they may be used for many products. Thus although specific features are important in most cases, almost all categories are affected by such attributes as ease of use. One general typology for evaluating new products is provided by Rogers (1983). By consistently using these or some other general attributes as well as specific features, the general impact of ease of use on eventual trial or market share can be estimated. These estimates in turn can provide guidance to R&D efforts and help in forecasting new product sales. By contrast, the use of specific features (for example, "frame buffer") will almost never lead to easy generalization.

Finally, every analysis plan should include an attempt to learn more about the market. Thus it is desirable to vary ways of measuring marketing variables (such as promotion) in a given study so that better estimates of their marginal effects can be developed.

Needs for Future Research

There are several promising avenues for future research on meta-analysis. Included are possibilities for Bayesian applications, potential refinements in estimation procedures, and more basic issues as well.

Bayesian Application of Meta-Analysis

The statistical approach used throughout this book has basically involved classical inference, chiefly because classical estimation was used in all of the models that provided the raw material for the meta-analyses. We have, however, flirted with Bayesian thinking by suggesting that tests of parameters from new work should use the mean or adjusted mean of parameters from existing work as the null hypothesis, rather than using the traditional null hypotheses of no effect or zero values of parameters.

There are situations, however, in which a more formal Bayesian approach to estimation may provide a major aid, particularly when data are sparse or when preliminary estimates are needed. For example, the Bass (1969) model of diffusion tends to be unstable when estimated early in product history when few data points are available, often producing infeasible estimates implying eternal growth for the product. In application, early estimates of upper bounds of market potential are among the most important benefits of forecasting applications of the diffusion model.

When parameters of the model must be estimated using just the first four or five data points, an appropriate procedure might be to use a prediction from a meta-analytic model with design variables configured as close to the current problem as possible as a prior estimate. Bayesian regression can then be used to get modified estimates of the coefficients of innovation and imitation, with updating done as new observations come in. Such a procedure would be more likely to give plausible early results, and it also uses available information more efficiently than does classical application-by-application estimation.

Estimation Problems: Possible Dependence of Errors in Meta-Analysis

The MANOVA model used to assess the Fishbein models took account of possible correlation of errors over the three parameters from each study. Otherwise parameters of all the other meta-analysis models were estimated with OLS methods—robust but not necessarily efficient or unbiased. Interest is now evident in estimation issues that might result from violations of assumptions of independence and homoscedasticity that underlie OLS estimation (Houston and Parsons 1986).

In our view, these problems will not prove nearly as serious as those autocorrelation problems that plague econometric models using time-series data. We also conjecture that problems related to defects in the natural experimental designs discussed in chapter 4 will be much more important, but research on estimation problems associated with meta-analysis could nonetheless prove useful and constructive.

The two principal problems identified so far are (1) heteroscedasticity in the estimated parameters that go into the meta-analysis and (2) potential problems caused by multiple use of the same data set by several authors and/or by use in meta-analysis of multiple results from a single study. In each case, relatively simple standard statistical approaches are available, but special problems that characterize meta-analysis will generally preclude their direct application. We are confident, however, that many other potential problems with estimation of parameters in meta-analysis models lurk undetected. We are now investigating two such problems, although we are sure that we will find others.

1) Unequal variances of estimated parameters that constitute the inputs to meta-analysis.

It is no surprise that some studies provide more reliable estimates of structural parameters than others—that is, that variances associated with estimates of a given parameter may vary over studies. When standard errors of the coefficients are reported, a straightforward weighted least-squares procedure can be used to improve efficiency. Unfortunately, the standard errors (or the equivalent t statistics) are often unreported in the studies used in a meta-analysis, although reasonable approximations may be available from reported significance levels or p values. Of course, weighting observations requires elimination of those observations for which no such estimates of variability are available, probably increasing problems with the experimental design.

2) Possibly correlated blocks of errors.

There is considerable recycling of data in many literatures—as, for example, repeated use of the Lydia Pinkham time series (starting with Palda 1964) in various reincarnations of distributed lag models. Further, most meta-analyses use more than one version of a model or more than one set of results from a given study. For example, the 113 elasticities used in the buyer behavior meta-analysis were produced by only 4 studies, and the 128 values of the econometrically estimated short-term advertising elasticities came from 28 studies. Several studies using the same data or several results from the same study may cause within-data or within-study blocks of residuals from the meta-analysis model to be correlated. In principal, this problem is easily dealt with, either by specifying a nondiagonal correlation structure for the residuals or by adding dummy variables to the meta-analysis design that correspond to these data or study blocks. Unfortunately, the design variables in the meta-analysis tend to block in much the same way as the additional data and study variables would block. The reason is simple: a given author in a given study tends to be committed to particular research technologies and particular research environments. The author may similarly be committed to a research technology over studies. The result of adding these new blocking variables will inevitably inject yet another unwelcome source of shared variance into the meta-analysis. At worst, the design variables and the study and data variables will be totally redundant, requiring many of the complex steps described in chapters 4 and 6. Currently this looks like the most interesting methodological estimation issue in meta-analysis. Our view is that a precedence analysis of the type described in chapter 6 is the most promising approach, with the research design and research environment variables viewed as precedent to the common data and author effects.

Basic Research Needs for the Future

A number of more basic developments would be useful. First, a more systematic investigation of the impact of model misspecification would be useful because this seems to be the most important cause of interstudy differences. This can be done by systematic testing of various specifications on given bodies of data rather than requiring new data for each test. Second, the statistical approaches used so far in meta- analysis have only scratched the surface of available possibilities for statistical creativity. Third, we would be pleased if more substantive areas were opened to meta-analytic scrutiny and if results from these various fields could be linked in a useful way. Fourth, extensions of ways to generate reasonable nonzero prior-posterior hypotheses would be useful, as would more orderly methods for setting up a natural experimental design to support a research program.

Finally, there may be a tendency for the clustering of measurement, estimation, and environment to become more pronounced as an established research paradigm emerges in a field. While convergence to a true model and appropriate method are desirable, there is a risk that convergence will be toward another point instead. From a meta-analytic point of view, a set of studies from such an established paradigm may constitute almost a single point in an experimental design. Even in these settings, then, an occasional test of a nonconventional sort may be useful to check for appropriate convergence.

References

Alpert, Bernard. 1967. "Non-Businessmen as Surrogates for Businessmen in Behavioral Experiments." *Journal of Business* 40:203-207.

Armstrong, J. Scott and Edward J. Lusk. 1985. "An Application of Meta-Analysis to Survey Research: The Effect of Return Postage." Working paper. Philadelphia: Wharton School, University of Pennsylvania.

Assmus, Gert, John U. Farley, and Donald R. Lehmann. 1984. "How Advertising Affects Sales: Meta-Analysis of Econometric Results." *Journal of Marketing Research* 21 (February):65-74.

Bagozzi, R.P. 1980. *Causal Models in Marketing.* New York: John Wiley.

Bass, Frank M. 1969. "A New Product Growth Model for Consumer Durables," *Management Science* 15 (January):215-227.

Bass, Frank M., Moshe M. Givon, Manohar U. Kalwani, David Reibstein, and Gordon P. Wright. 1984. "An Investigation into the Order to the Brand Choice Process." *Marketing Science* 3 (Fall):267-287.

Bass, Frank M., and Robert P. Leone. 1983. "Temporal Aggregations, the Data Interval Bias, and Empirical Estimation of Bimonthly Relations from Annual Data." *Management Science* 29(1):1-11.

Bass, Frank M., and William L. Wilkie. 1973. "A Comparative Analysis of Attitudinal Predictions of Brand Preference." *Journal of Marketing Research* 10:262-269.

Black, Timothy R.L., and John U. Farley. 1977. "An Awareness-Knowledge-Trial Model of a Kenyan Contraceptive Test Market." *Journal of Advertising Research* 17 (October):49-56.

Bock, R. Darrell. 1975. *Multivariate Statistical Methods Behavioral Research.* New York: McGraw-Hill.

Bolton, Ruth N., and Randall G. Chapman. 1984. "An Audit of Structural Equation Modeling Applications in Marketing." In Russell W. Belk et al., *1984 AMA Educators' Proceedings.* Chicago: American Marketing Association.

Brinberg, David, and James Jaccard. 1986. "A Review of Meta-Analytic Techniques." In Richard J. Lutz, ed., *Advances in Consumer Research.* Vol. 13. Provo, Utah: Association for Consumer Research:606-611.

Campbell, Donald T., and Donald W. Fiske. 1959. "Convergent Discriminant Validity by the Multitrait-Multidimensional Matrix." *Psychological Bulletin* 56 (March): 81-105.

Capon, Noel, John U. Farley, and Donald R. Lehmann. 1985. "A Methodology for the Study of Organizational and Environmental Contingencies." Working paper. New York: Columbia University.

Carpenter, Gregory, and John U. Farley. 1984. "Estimating Parameter Shifts in Simultaneous Equation Models." Working paper. New York: Columbia University.

Cattin, Philippe, and Dick R. Wittink. 1983. "Commercial Use of Conjoint Analysis: A Survey." *Journal of Marketing* 46 (Summer):44-53.

Charlton, Peter. 1973. "A Review of Shop Loyalty," *Journal of Market Research Society* 15(1):35-51.

Chatfield, C., A.S.C. Ehrenberg, and G.J. Goodhardt. 1966. "Progress on a Simplified Model of Stationary Purchasing Behavior." *Journal of the Royal Statistical Society*, ser. A, 129:317-367.

Chatfield, C., and G.J. Goodhardt. 1970. "The Beta-Binomial Model for Consumer Purchasing Behavior." *Applied Statistics*, C, 19(3)240-250.

———. 1973. "A Consumer Purchasing Model with Erlang Inter-purchase Times." *Journal of the American Statistical Association* 68:828-835.

———. 1975. "Results Concerning Brand Choice," *Journal of Marketing Research* 12:110-113.

Churchill, Gilbert A., Jr., Neil M. Ford, Steven W. Hartley, and Orville C. Walker, Jr. 1985. "The Determinants of Salesperson Performance: A Meta-Analysis." *Journal of Marketing Research* 22 (May):103-118.

Churchill, Gilbert A., and J. Paul Peter. 1984. "Research Design Effects on the Reliability of Rating Scales: A Meta-Analysis." *Journal of Marketing Research* 21 (November):360-375.

Clarke, Darral G. 1976. "Econometric Measurement of the Duration of Advertising Effect on Sales." *Journal of Marketing Research* 13 (November):345-357.

Clarke, Darral G., and John M. McCann. 1973. "Measuring the Cumulative Effects of Advertising: A Reappraisal." Chicago: *Proceedings of American Marketing Association*.

Claycamp, Henry J., and Massy, William F. 1968. "A Theory of Market Segmentation." *Journal of Marketing Research* 5:388-394.

Comanor, William S., and Thomas A. Wilson. 1974. *Advertising and Market Power*. Cambridge: Harvard University Press.

Dorfman, Robert, and Peter O. Steiner. 1954. "Optimal Advertising and Optimal Quality." *American Economic Review* 44 (December):826-836.

Draper, N., and H. Smith. 1966. *Applied Regression Analysis*. New York: John Wiley & Sons.

Dutka, Solomon. 1984. "Combining Tests of Significance in Test Marketing Research Experiments." *Journal of Marketing Research* 21 (February):118-119.

Ehrenberg, A.S.C. 1959. "The Patterns of Consumer Purchases." *Applied Statistics* 8:26-41.

———. 1965. "An Appraisal of Markov Brand Switching Models." *Journal of Marketing Research* 2 (November):347-362.

———. 1972. *Repeat Buying: Theory and Application*. Amsterdam: North-Holland.

———. 1975a. *Data Reduction*. New York: John Wiley.

————. 1975b. "The Structure of an Industrial Market: Aviation Fuel Contract."*Industrial Marketing Management* 4:273-285.

Ehrenberg, A.S.C., and G.J. Goodhardt. 1970. "A Model of Multi-Brand Buying." *Journal of Marketing Research* 7 (February):77-84.

————. 1976. "Decision Models and Descriptive Models in Marketing." *Marketing Science Institute.* Cambridge, Mass.

————. 1979. "The Dirichlet Model." In *Understanding Buyer Behavior.* New York: J.W. Thompson & M.R.C.A.

Farley, John U. 1967. "Estimating Structural Parameters of Marketing Systems." In *1967 Summer Conference Proceedings.* Edited by Reed Moyer. Chicago: American Marketing Association.

Farley, John U., and Melvin J. Hinich. 1970. "Detecting 'Small' Mean Shifts in Time Series." *Management Science* 17:189-199.

Farley, John U., Melvin J. Hinich, and Timothy W. McGuire. 1975. "Some Comparisons of Tests for the Shift in the Slopes of a Multivariate Linear Time Series Model." *Journal of Econometrics* 3:297-318.

Farley, John U., and John A. Howard. 1975. *Control of "Error" in Market Research Data.* Lexington, Mass.: Lexington Books.

Farley, John U., John A. Howard, and Donald R. Lehmann. 1976. "A Working Version Car Buyer-Behavior Model." *Management Science* 23 (November):235-247.

————. 1974. "Evaluating Test Market Results: Buyer Behavior Analysis in Argentina." *Journal of Business Administration* 5 (Spring):69-88.

Farley, John U., J.R. Katz, and D.R. Lehmann. 1977. "Patterns in Repeated Attitude Measurements on New and Established Brands of Subcompact Cars." Working paper. New York: Columbia University.

————. 1978. "Impact of Different Sets of Comparison Brands on Evaluation of a New Subcompact Car Brand." *Journal of Consumer Research* 5 (September):138-143.

Farley, John U., J.R. Katz, D.R. Lehmann, and R.S. Winer. 1979. "Two Approaches to Enriching Specifications of Consumer Decision Process Models." *Proceeding*, First Annual TIMS/ORSA Conference on Market Measurement, Stanford University.

Farley, John U., Donald R. Lehmann, and Terrence A. Oliva. 1985. "Are There Laws in Production? Cobb-Douglas Revisited." Working paper. New York: Columbia University.

Farley, John U., Donald R. Lehmann, and Michael J. Ryan. 1981. "Generalizing from Imperfect Replication." *Journal of Business* 54 (October):597-610.

————. 1982. "Patterns in Parameters of Buyer Behavior Models: Generalization from Sparse Replication." *Marketing Science* 1 (Spring):181-204.

Farley, John U., Donald R. Lehmann, Russell S. Winer, and Jerrold Katz. 1982. "Parameter Stationarity and 'Carry-Over Effects' in a Consumer Decision Process Model." *Journal of Consumer Research* 8 (March):465-471.

Farley, John U., and Srinivas Reddy. 1985. "A Factorial Evaluation of Effects of Misspecification and Noise on Estimation in Structural Equation Models." Working paper. New York: Columbia University.

Farley, John U., and L.W. Ring. 1970. "An Empirical Test of the Howard-Sheth Model of Buyer Behavior." *Journal of Marketing Research* 7 (November):427-438.

————. 1972. "On L and R and HAPPISM." *Journal of Marketing Research* 9 (August):349-353.

————. 1974. " 'Empirical' Specification of a Buyer Behavior Model." *Journal of Marketing Research* 11 (February):89-96.

Farley, John U., and Donald E. Sexton. 1982. "A Process Model of the Family Planning Decision." *TIMS Studies in Management Science* 18:209-239.

Ferber, Robert. 1977. "Research by Convenience," *Journal of Consumer Research* 4:57-58.

Fishbein, Martin, and Icek Ajzen. 1975. *Belief, Attitude, Intention and Behavior: An Introduction to Theory and Research*. Reading, Mass.: Addison-Wesley.

Fishburn, Peter C., and Gary A. Kochenberger. 1979. "Two-Piece Von Neuman-Morgenstern Utility Functions." *Decision Sciences* 10:503-518.

Frank, Ronald E., William F. Massy, and Yoram Wind. 1975. *Market Segmentation*. Englewood Cliffs, N.J.: Prentice-Hall.

Green, Paul, Douglas Carroll, and Wayne DeSarbo. 1978. "A New Measurement of Predictor Variable Importance in Multiple Regression." *Journal of Marketing Research* 15 (August):356-360.

Glass, Gene V., Barry McGaw, and Mary Lee Smith. 1981. *Meta-Analysis in Social Research*. Beverly Hills: Sage.

Goodhardt, G.J. 1976. *Fitting the Dirichlet Model*. London: Aske Research.

Goodhardt, G.J., and C.R. Chatfield. 1973. "Gamma Distribution in Consumer Purchasing." *Nature* 244:316.

Goodhardt, G.J., A.S.C. Ehrenberg, and M.A. Collins. 1975. *The Television Audience: Patterns of Viewing*. London: Saxon House.

Gruber, Robert E. 1978. "The Impact of Response Style and Response Set on Large Scale Survey Research Involving Activity, Interest and Opinion (AIO) Variables." Ph.D. dissertation, Columbia University.

Hauser, John R., and Steven P. Gaskin. 1984. "Application of the 'Defenders' Consumer Model," *Marketing Science* 2 (Fall):327-351.

Hauser, John R., and Steven M. Shugan. 1983. "Defensive Marketing Strategies." *Marketing Science* 2 (Fall):319-360.

Hedges, Larry V., and Ingram Olkin. 1985. *Statistical Methods for Meta-Analysis*. Orlando, Fl.: Academic Press.

Houston, Franklin, and Leonard Parsons. 1986. "Meta-Analysis Using Econometric Methods." Presented at TIMS Marketing Science Conference, University of Texas, Dallas, March.

Houston, Franklin, and Doyle L. Weiss. 1974. "An Analysis of Competitive Market Behavior." *Journal of Marketing Research* 11 (March):151-155.

Houston, Michael J., J. Paul Peter, and Alan G. Sawyer. 1983. "The Role of Meta-Analysis in Consumer Research." In Richard P. Bagozzi and Alice M. Tybout, eds., *Advances in Consumer Research*. Vol. 10. Ann Arbor, Mich.: Association for Consumer Research.

Howard, J.A., and J.N. Sheth. 1969. *The Theory of Buyer Behavior*. New York: John Wiley.

Hunter, John E., Frank L. Schmidt, and Gregg B. Jackson. 1982. *Meta-Analysis: Cumulating Research Findings across Studies*. Beverly Hills: Sage.

Joreskog, K.G. and D. Sorborm. 1977. "Statistical Models for Analysis of Longitudinal Data." In D.J. Aigner and A.S. Goldberger, *Latent Variables in Socioeconomic Models*. Amsterdam: North-Holland Publishing.

Kalwani, Manohar V., and Alvin J. Silk. 1982. "On the Reliability and Predictive Validity of Purchase Intention Measures." *Marketing Science* 1 (Summer):243-286.

Kassarjian, Harold, H. 1971. "Personality and Consumer Behavior: A Review." *Journal of Marketing Research* 8 (November):409-419.

Kau Ah Keng, and Andrew Ehrenberg. 1984. "Patterns of Store Choice." *Journal of Marketing Research* 21 (November):399-409.

Lastovicka, John L. 1982. "On the Validation of Lifestyle Traits: A Review and Illustration." *Journal of Marketing Research* 19 (February):126-138.

Leff, Nathaniel, and John U. Farley. 1980. "Advertising and Development." *Journal of International Business Studies* 11 (Fall):65-79.

Lehmann, Donald R., and John U. Farley. 1981. "Decomposing the Correlation Matrix in Panel Data." In *Advances in Consumer Research* 8. Edited by Kent Monroe. Washington: Association for Consumer Research.

Leone, Robert P., and Randall L. Schultz. 1980. "A Study of Marketing Generalizations." *Journal of Marketing* 44 (Winter):10-18.

Little, John D.C. 1975. "BRANDAID: A Marketing Mix Model, Part I: Structure; Part II: Implementation." *Operations Research* 23:628-673.

Maddala, G.S., and R.G. Vogel. 1969. "Estimating Lagged Relationship in Corporate Demand for Liquid Assets." *Review of Economics and Statistics* 51 (February):53-61.

Mahajan, Vijay, Eitan Muller, and Subash Sharma. 1984. "An Empirical Comparison of Awareness Forecasting Models of New Product Introduction." *Marketing Science* 3 (Summer):179-197.

Mayer, Charles S. 1974. "Data Collection Methods: Personal Interviews." In *Handbook of Marketing Research*. Edited by Robert Ferber. New York: McGraw-Hill.

Monroe, Kent B., and R. Krishnan. 1983. "A Procedure for Integrating Outcomes Across Studies." In Richard P. Bagozzi and Alice M. Tybout, eds., *Advances in Consumer Research*. Vol. 10. Ann Arbor, Mich.: Association for Consumer Research.

Nelson, Philip. 1974. "Information and Consumer Behavior." *Journal of Political Economy* 78:311-329.

Palda, Kristian S. 1964. *The Measurement of Cumulative Advertising Effects*. Englewood Cliffs, N.J.: Prentice-Hall.

Parsons, Leonard J. 1975. "The Product Life Cycle and Time-Varying Advertising Elasticities." *Journal of Marketing Research* 12 (November):476-480.

————. 1976. "A Ratchet Model of Advertising Carryover Effects." *Journal of Marketing Research* 13 (February):76-79.

Payne, Stanley L. 1974. "Data Collection Methods: Telephone Surveys." In *Handbook of Marketing Research*. Edited by Robert Ferber. New York: McGraw-Hill.

Peter, J. Paul, and Gilbert A. Churchill. 1984. "The Relationships among Research Design Choices and Psychometric Properties of Rating Scales: A Meta-Analysis." University of Wisconsin Working Paper 8-84-13.

Peterson, Robert A., Gerald Albaum, and Richard P. Beltramini. 1975. "A Meta-Analysis of Effect Sizes in Consumer Behavior Experiments." *Journal of Consumer Research* 12 (June):97-103.

Ray, Michael L. 1979. "Introduction to the Special Section: Measurement and Marketing Research—Is the Flirtation Going to Lead to a Romance?" *Journal of Marketing Research* 16:1-16.

Reibstein, David J., John Bateson, and William Boulding. 1983. "A Framework for Assessing the Reliability of Conjoint Analysis." Working paper. Philadelphia: Wharton School, University of Pennsylvania.

Reilly, Michael D., and Jerry D. Conover. 1983. "Meta-Analysis: Integrating Results from Consumer Research Studies." In Richard P. Bagozzi and Alice M. Tybout, eds., *Advances in Consumer Research*. Vol. 10. Ann Arbor, Mich.: Association for Consumer Research.

Rogers, E.M. 1983. *Diffusion of Innovations*. New York: Free Press.

Rosenthal, Robert. 1979. "The 'File Drawer Problem' and Tolerance for Null Results." *Psychological Bulletin* 83 (March):638-641.

Runkel, Philips J., and Joseph E. McGrath. 1972. *Research on Human Behavior: A Systematic Guide to Method*. New York: Holt, Rinehart & Winston.

Ryan, Michael J., and Donald W. Barclay. 1983. "Integrating Results from Independent Studies." In Richard P. Bagozzi and Alice M. Tybout, eds., *Advances in Consumer Research*. Vol. 10. Ann Arbor, Mich.: Association for Consumer Research.

Ryan, Michael J., and E.H. Bonfield. 1975. "The Fishbein Extended Model and Consumer Behavior." *Journal of Consumer Research* 2:118-136.

Ryan, Michael J., and Michael J. Etzel. 1976. "The Nature of Salient Outcomes and Referents in the Extended Model." In M.J. Schlinger, ed., *Advances in Consumer Research*. Vol. 3. Chicago: Association for Consumer Research.

Salipante, Paul, William Notz, and John Bigelow. 1982. "A Matrix Approach to Literature Reviews." *Research in Organizational Behavior* 4:321-348.

Schultz, Randall L., and Robert P. Leone. 1980. "A Study of Marketing Generalizations," *Journal of Marketing* 44 (Winter):10-18.

Sheth, Jagdish N. 1970. "Are there Differences in Dissonance Reduction Behavior between Students and Housewives?" *Journal of Marketing Research* 7:243-245.

Sternthal, Brian, Alice M. Tybout, and Bobby J. Calder. 1986. "Methodological Issues and Theory Testing Research." Working Paper, Northwestern University.

Sudman, Seymour. 1964. "On the Accuracy of Recording of Consumer Panels: I and II. *Journal of Marketing Research* 1 (May):14-20; (August):69-83.

Telser, Lester G. 1962. "Advertising and Cigarettes," *Journal of Political Economy* 70 (October):471-99.

Urban, Glen L. 1970. "SPRINTER Mod. III: A Model for the Analysis of New Frequently Purchased Consumer Products." *Operations Research* 18 (September-October):805-854.

———. 1975. "PERCEPTOR: A Model for Product Positioning." *Management Science* 21 (April):858-871.

Urban, Glen L., and Gerald M. Katz. 1983. "Pre-Test Market Models' Validation and Managerial Implications." *Journal of Marketing Research* 20 (August):221-234.

Vanhonacker, Wilfried. 1982. "Temporal Aggregation and Finite Parameter Efficiency

Assuming First-Order Serial Correlation." Working paper. New York: Columbia University.

Weinstein, David, and John U. Farley. 1974. "Market Segmentation and Parameter Inequalities in a Buyer Behavior Model." *Journal of Business* 48:526-540.

Wells, William D. 1975. "Psychographics: A Critical Review." *Journal of Marketing Research* 12 (May):196-213.

Wiseman, Frederick. 1979. "Noncontact and Refusal Rates in Consumer Telephone Surveys." *Journal of Marketing Research* 16 (November):478-484.

Wilkie, William L., and Edgar A. Pessemier. 1973. "Issues in Marketing's Use of Multiattribute Models." *Journal of Marketing Research* 10:428-441.

Yu, Julie, and Harris Cooper. 1983. "A Quantitative Review of Research Design Effects on Response Rates to Questionnaires." *Journal of Marketing Research* 20 (February):36-44.

Index

About the Authors

John U. Farley, R.C. Kopf Professor of International Marketing at the Graduate School of Business, Columbia University, is Executive Director of the Marketing Science Institute. A graduate of Dartmouth in Russian, Dr. Farley received an M.B.A. from the Amos Tuck School in finance and statistics, and a Ph.D. from the University of Chicago in marketing, statistics, and economics. A member of the Columbia faculty since 1970, Dr. Farley has also taught at Carnegie-Mellon University; Handelshogskolan, Gothenburg, Sweden; London Graduate School of Business Studies; Massachusetts Institute of Technology; Dartmouth College; INSEAD Fontainebleau, France; and the National University of Singapore. He has published in, and served on the editorial boards of a variety of professional journals, including *Marketing Science, Journal of Marketing,* and *Journal of Marketing Research.*

Donald R. Lehmann is the George E. Warren Professor of Business and the Coordinator of the Ph.D. program at Columbia University's Graduate School of Business. He has also taught at Cornell and NYU. He holds a B.S. in mathematics from Union College in Schenectady, New York, and an MSIA and Ph.D. from the Krannert School of Management at Purdue. He has done research in the areas of individual and group decision making, multivariate statistical methods, and the impact of planning and strategy on performance. His publications include *Market Research and Analysis,* in addition to numerous articles in professional journals. He serves on the editorial board of *Journal of Marketing, Journal of Marketing Research, Journal of Consumer Research,* and *Marketing Science.*